QUEER CALLINGS

Queer Callings

UNTIMELY NOTES ON NAMES AND DESIRES

Mark D. Jordan

FORDHAM UNIVERSITY PRESS   NEW YORK 2024

Fordham University Press has no responsibility for the
persistence or accuracy of URLs for external or third-
party Internet websites referred to in this publication and
does not guarantee that any content on such websites is,
or will remain, accurate or appropriate.

Fordham University Press also publishes its books in a
variety of electronic formats. Some content that appears
in print may not be available in electronic books.

Visit us online at www.fordhampress.com.

Library of Congress Cataloging-in-Publication Data
available online at https://catalog.loc.gov.

Printed in the United States of America

26 25 24   5 4 3 2 1

First edition

Contents

QUEER CALLINGS

Prologue:
Our Names, Our Destinies!

> JACK: But you don't really mean to say that you couldn't love me if my name wasn't Ernest?
>
> GWENDOLEN: But your name *is* Ernest.
>
> JACK: Yes, I know it is. But supposing it was something else? Do you mean to say you couldn't love me then?
>
> GWENDOLEN: Ah! that is clearly a metaphysical speculation, and like all metaphysical speculations has very little reference at all to the actual facts of real life, as we know them.
>
> —OSCAR WILDE,
> *THE IMPORTANCE OF BEING EARNEST*, ACT 1[1]

Wilde's relentless farce mocks romance, marriage, church, class, and naming—but especially naming, which crosses all the others. As you may remember and could guess from the quotation, some of Wilde's characters like to invent names for themselves. The script labels one of them "Jack," but he is known as "Ernest" to London society and to his beloved,

Gwendolen. From a tender age, she has decided that she can only love someone by the name of Ernest. She loves *by means of* the name. She claims now to love this particular (so-called) Ernest—the one Wilde identifies as Jack. She rejects as "metaphysical speculation" any question about loving him under another name. Alas, "the actual facts of real life" that she knows are wrong. Or maybe not. After many twists, Jack's legal name—John Worthington—will be revealed as the haphazard labeling of the kind-hearted philanthropist who adopted him from a railway package room. John, the blandest of English forenames. "Worthington," the destination on the left-luggage ticket. If loving a "John" would shatter Gwendolen's ideal, the randomness of "Worthington" is an insuperable social obstacle for her mother. Lady Bracknell cannot permit her daughter to marry a nameless foundling who cannot recite a pedigree. Happily, Jack's true origins are revealed in the play's final act: He comes from an acceptable family (a branch of Lady Bracknell's own), and he was christened Ernest, after his father. Jack's name is "Ernest after all . . . it naturally is Ernest" (537).

An ending fit for romantic comedy: fantasies of love fulfilled, the social order confirmed, our hero's lies reinterpreted as premonitions of truth. But the play's final rejoicing cannot hide how many troubles it has raised for any romance that counts on names. We might retitle the play "The Trouble with Names" or just "Naming Trouble." Whatever the final curtain's version of the facts, grandly metaphysical speculation about natural naming is wrong on two counts. No name is imposed by nature, and no name can capture whatever people or things actually are.

Consider the confidence, shared by Gwendolen and Cecily (her counterpart), that seekers after true love can know in advance the first names of their soulmates. They rely on names as others do on astrological signs: to choose partners or friends, to reenchant daily life with cosmic fates. Like astral archetypes, names are supposed to foretell destinies. Without ever having seen him, Cecily can record in a diary the plot of romance with *her* Ernest—long before she has met the adorable body wearing that name. Her scented pages already depict heart-racing encounters, bitter ruptures, a culminating proposal. Of course, in Wilde's play, when Cecily meets *her* Ernest his (real?) name is Algernon or Algy. No matter: Nominal destiny triumphs over inconvenient circumstance and human foibles. For both Gwendolen and Cecily, names promise happy endings. Gwendolen declares, early on, "My ideal has always been to love someone of the name Ernest. There is something in the name that inspires absolute confidence" (490). She treats "Ernest" as a common name before it becomes personal. It applies to an individual only as the specimen of a kind. Gwendolen must marry an Ernest, but most any Ernest will do: "The moment Algernon first mentioned to me that he had a friend called Ernest, I knew I was destined to love you." Love at first hearing.

The trouble with this ideal, as the play keeps showing, is that names can be lies—or, to speak more accurately, fictions. Jack has invented a younger brother named "Ernest" and placed him in London so that he can have a regular excuse to visit the city. Once there, Jack puts on the fiction of Ernest and offers calling cards to prove it. His friend, Algernon, has meanwhile conjured up an invalid named "Bunbury." Poor Bunbury's unpredictable ailments allow Algernon (aka Algy) to evade awkward dinner invitations by pleading an urgent trip to care for his sick friend somewhere in the country. When Algy really does leave London to search out Cecily, he appropriates one of Jack's fictitious calling cards to become a duplicate Ernest. (Same species-tag, different specimen.) Far from inspiring "absolute confidence," the name is a portable fiction. No Ernest is earnest, and even calling cards lie.

How to avert chaos in courtship? The play appeals to a churchly sacrament of naming. Jack is revealed to be "naturally" Ernest because he was baptized as an infant with the "Christian name" of his father, General Moncrieff. Lady Bracknell can summon firsthand testimony of the ritual, since Jack's deceased mother is now revealed as her sister, Algernon's mother: "Every luxury that money could buy, including christening, had been lavished on you. . . . Being the eldest son you were naturally christened after your father" (537). Since Lady Bracknell cannot recall the general's first names, it takes a few minutes and a handy set of army directories to establish them: Ernest John. (First names are curiously private in the play. We learn several of them only in its final minutes, but others never. Servants labor still behind their surnames.) Lady Bracknell's testimony presumes that baptism is a luxury good and that the religious names bestowed by it are correctly determined by patriarchal succession. Worse: Her testimony takes place at a meeting arranged to baptize Jack and possibly Algy into other names—without a religious motive or any effort to feign one. That is the extent of Jack's being "naturally" Ernest.

In Wilde's play, other types of names shift by picking up unexpected meanings. Consider place names, for example. Jack rents out his house on the "unfashionable side" of Belgrave Square, but he—or his fictitious younger brother—lives while in London at the Albany, notable *bachelors'* quarters or "sets." "Bachelor" was often a euphemism. The play's final episode is a sort of double date in which two bachelor friends find suitable women for marriage. The date turns out to be almost incestuous: Jack (sometimes Ernest) is an older brother to Algy (only rarely Ernest). Gwendolen is a first cousin to Algy—and so to Jack. Cecily, the young woman she has just started calling "sister," is Jack's ward. Wife-cousin, best-friend brothers, "sister" sister-in-law. A worrisome jumble of marital roles puts an end to bachelorhood—or maybe not.

One other name hovered over the play's first performances: "sodomite"—or "somdomite," as the Marquess of Queensberry misspelled it on the public accusation he delivered to Wilde's club four days after the theatrical premiere. Originally a place name (see Genesis 19), "sodomite" became over centuries a Christian indictment against a type of sinner—on some accounts, the archsinner. Wilde's play never utters the damning slur, of course, even when it winks at current stereotypes associated with it. The opening stage directions describe Algernon's apartment as "luxuriously and artistically furnished." We find him—or hear him—playing the piano, and we learn later that he has a fondness for scandalous "French songs" (480, 489). Algernon remarks on "the extraordinary number of bachelors one sees all over the place" (483). He adds, some minutes later, "In married life three is company and two is none" (487)—without specifying the gender of the third. And so on. Of course, Algernon must marry Cecily as Jack marries Gwendolen. No words describe this compulsory "heterosexuality" (a word just then migrating from German to English). The play's witticisms at the expense of romance and marriage offer no names, common or proper, for the assumption of the universality of male-female attraction.

Pause for a moment over the conventions around which Wilde can generate so much trouble. How variously do you name yourself in still running comedies of solitude, desire, love, and marriage? How many calling cards do you need to order from the printer—or online dating apps? What destinies might you wish each name to announce—or what amorous fates convey? And which authorities do you trust to determine "the actual facts of real life" as you now profess to know them?

If it is easy to laugh with Wilde's first audiences at the characters' foibles, it is not always so easy to joke at our own schemes for naming love—say, the requirement that we each claim a sexual identity.

As you finished that last sentence, you may have braced for another complaint against "identity politics." You need not worry. I find that lumping all identities together only misleads us into thinking that they are equivalent *as identities*. In this book, I pull "sexual identities" and "gender identities" away from the rest of identity-language. Doing that is hard enough—and surprisingly controversial. Still, I hope to show that an earnest reliance on them is only the latest episode in a long campaign to shrink sex/gender variation to the limits of confident knowingness. If this knowingness can be politically useful or psychologically comforting for a while, it can also and quickly enough turn vengeful.

Here is another challenge. I hope to lift questions about sex/gender names away from our current practice or malpractice of politics. Speaking our complex experiences of bodily desires or loves is not only or even chiefly a political matter. Erotic speech may well lie at the opposite pole from the mediatized polemic we now call "politics." This book shows how we might speak sex/gender otherwise. It is like a (camp) love song in the middle of stridently literal social critique—like that duet by Polly and Mack the Knife in *The Threepenny Opera*: "Love lasts or it doesn't/In this place or any other."[2] When he finishes the couplet, Mack heads off to more conquests, leaving Polly with soiled fantasies and a trampled heart. Still, for a few bars, the song sounds a lyrical possibility that it can barely foresee. Try reading this book not as another op-ed but as a dream-recital of imaginary languages.

My suspicion of "the actual facts of real life" presumed by our current names must have many autobiographical sources, most of them concealed from me. Still, I can tell you two origin stories.

The first is comfortably academic. For decades, I have read Michel Foucault.[3] He often expresses skepticism about notions like "sexual identity." Sometimes he associates that phrase with official documents. Speaking to a French conference in 1979, he objects: "Pleasure is something that passes from one individual to another; it is not the secretion of identity. Because pleasure has no passport, no identity card."[4] At other times, Foucault suggests that contemporary notions of identity both resemble and displace Christian doctrines about soul. He introduces one book, *Discipline and Punish*, as "a correlative history of the *modern soul* and of a new power to judge."[5] The modern soul is designed as the target needed by modern bureaucracies. To install themselves, recently proclaimed powers contort the old body into shapes easier for them to grip. They overwrite libraries of religious speech. The modern soul co-opts the Christian soul—edits its names and characteristics without quite forgetting it.

For many Christian theologies, my soul is at once my deepest self and my link to every other human creature. It is at once the ground of community and the unique moral record by which I alone will be judged. The modern Euro-American soul inherits from Christian theology the notion of soul as both an individual tag and a species, a serial number and a product line, a (possibly dubious) personal history and a (stable but threatened) kind. The two are linked through the notion of identity.

There are, of course, counters to Foucault's objections against modern identity. If vernacular Marxisms emphasize class consciousness or ideological stages, minoritized voices have reclaimed not just individual variation but the layering of multiple identities onto a single body. No, all gay men are *not* the same *as* gay men: Some gay men benefit from other attributes counted socially valuable (Whiteness, gender conformity, money in the bank), while others are loaded with further burdens of social devaluation. In recent decades, people often abbreviate this sort of counterclaim by speaking of "intersectionality." Unfortunately, intersectionality can be misunderstood as the *sum* of different identity markers, each identical to other markers of the same kind and all identical as identities. But we falsify our punishing or privileging divisions when we treat them as coordinate numbers on a universal grid. The reduction of intersectionality to a sum is roughly the opposite of what earlier writers like Audre Lorde or Kimberlé Crenshaw meant. In some current uses of "intersectionality," and against their intentions, a simplified logic of identity-sameness displaces acute perceptions of the complexity of human difference.

Hoping to step away from the back-and-forth of repetitive quarrels, I notice something else: Even though sharp critiques of sexual or gender "identity" started up just as soon as the term passed into general use, they did not slow its spread. The most famous critics were cited piously and then ignored. That gives more than enough grounds for a little suspicion. Suspicion about dogmatic labeling is what I mean to encourage. I have no desire to ban phrases about sex/gender identity. I suggest rather that we surround them with other styles of naming to increase multilingualism while reinforcing awareness of the many kinds of meaning that encircle the literal.

There you have the first origin story about my suspicion of current language for sex and gender, ornamented with a few Foucauldian applications. Here's the second, which is less academic and harder for me to tell. Several years ago, my last parent died. I began to experience a loss of voice that I could only conceive as "aphonia"—in honor of the woman Freud named "Dora" when he published (or betrayed) her case. Apparently I too wanted some "unsaid" to be "lost, in the body, between bodies."[6] My family's story, now populated by ghosts, is no part of this book. My symptom may be.

I lost my voice most often in committee meetings on campus. After a few embarrassing episodes, I learned to take a combination of prescribed pills at least forty-five minutes in advance. Classes were less worrisome, since I could swim in the conversation after a few nervous minutes. Still, in other academic settings, the problem continued. I realized that my aphonia was also aphasia, that I would lose my voice but also my command of standard terminology. It was like "coming out": struggling, dry-mouthed, to say the dreaded words while wondering whether any words were adequate. How does "I love you"—as confession, seduction, poetic experiment—become the diagnostic and political declaration "I'm gay"?

After two or three years, as my voice reverted to "normal," I could not forget that my participation in the languages clamoring around me was itself ephemeral. I had gained it in the years after my birth and could lose it before my death. I had learned to speak and write; at any moment, I might be required to *re*learn. The recovered language need not be—*could* not be—exactly the language I had acquired as a child. As language clamors, it changes. So do its mortal speakers. Reentering language, I would have to choose anew—or comply with fresh assignments of—the kind of speaker I would now be.

In current societies, sex/gender language is more ephemeral even than the bodies it names. I performed a prescribed linguistic ritual when I "came out as gay." I accomplished another when I began to speak of my "sexual identity," which both assumed and reinforced a "gender identity." The specifics of those stages place my micro-history of language learning within much larger shifts in the versions of English around me. In this book, I do sketch some of those *macro*-histories. Still, since my little episode of aphonia/aphasia, I cannot forget that names are applied by and to individual bodies within mortal micro-histories.

Any macro-history of human language rests on vulnerable bodies that speak (sing, sign, write). A fuller history of my use of sex/gender language would have to complicate macro-historical periodization with the particular scenes of my linguistic education. Where and when did I learn which terms? How many of them were "dirty words"? How much of my present sex/gender vocabulary should still count as slang? (If you judge the answers to such questions obvious, please try the experiment of writing some pages of your own linguistic history—for example, the first steps in your learning when and how to say "fuck.") Supposedly neutral, objective, comprehensive histories of English words are incomplete until they are cross-hatched with individual memories.

Debates around sex/gender languages can bully by abstraction unless they recognize the desirous intimacies of learning, unlearning, and relearning. The will to abstraction expresses itself in efforts to legislate a correct language for all, but it appears already in the assumption that any daily language is unitary and unchanging. Remind yourself that American English is not a single, fixed language. For many historical reasons, that reminder is especially pertinent to versions of English we might want to call "queer."

Fifteen or twenty years ago, I began asking members of trans groups in the Bay Area about their linguistic improvisations. The creativity of local variation astonished me. I would do an interview in the Mission District of San Francisco and think that I had grasped what was emerging. Then I would talk with someone from Oakland and hear a different set of pronouns, plots, and characters. No Academy was appointed to arbitrate the divergence. None was needed. Differences might cause small misunderstandings or momentary surprise. ("You still call yourself *that*?") Most misfires were absorbed into a larger play of co-creation and rivalry—as least, for those counted into the groups.

A few paragraphs back, I distinguished macro-frames of common terminologies for sex/gender from the microbiographies of their use by individuals. Something more complicated is hinted at in my use of "co-creation." Languages are shared, we sometimes insist, especially when we appeal to "common" usage. Historically, they have not been shared equally. Some speakers claim more authority to alter or enforce what is supposedly held in common. Some ways of speaking accrue more status or privilege. Of course, marginalized groups retain the capacity to remake language by slang, jargon, argot—not to say, by acts of literature. These resistant languages are generated in dozens of ways, from obvious variation to wholesale importation of other vocabularies and grammars. What interests me now is not how the counterlanguage arises or how it might set its makers apart. Instead, I am curious about the resources backtalk offers for shifting how speakers are named.

During the decades of my studying and teaching, communities of dissident sex or gender renamed themselves regularly. Doing that, they continued a long history. Its stages are less important than the ongoing fussing over ways of naming. What lies behind it? Like any writer on sex/gender over the last four or five decades, I can trace linguistic shifts in my own writing. I began by using "homosexual" (even in my private journal) as an academically acceptable term with neutral content—or so I would have said if pressed. Of course, it was acceptable because condescending and neutral because overfamiliar. Whatever the reforming intentions of those who coined it, "homosexual" never moves far from the clinic or the police court. My writing turned next to "gay," mostly in phrases like "gay liberation" and its cousins. Then there was "queer," which I preferred for its old etymology and its elusiveness: From the sixteenth century on, it has meant strange, peculiar, eccentric, but also suspicious or doubtful (not least, with regard to good taste). Clinging to that etymology, I still use "queer" to refuse ordinary labeling—to scramble or twist language, to disclose its reserve of silence. But quickly enough, even in my own writing, "queer" became either an umbrella to cover the letters of the ever-expanding acronym or else another element within that list: LGBTQ. That standardization effaces the protest by "queer" against literalism—against the assumption that any combination of fixed names could be adequate to human sex/gender. Even as I cede to the changing diction, I continue to hope that "queer" can remain the opposite of the acronym. It is *not* a variable sum of things reduced to sameness under letter-labels.

Underneath the linguistic shift, I keep hearing a question about the primal scene of our naming. What do we think we are doing when we affix or remove names for our sex/gender? Are we revisiting the choice of a term from a fixed list of options? Or are we trying to recoin a (proper?) name for ourselves? "Ourselves," I say. Perhaps "my self." Either way, another set of questions lurks here, because it is unclear *what* I am trying to name. If there is some X underneath "homosexual," "invert," "homophile," "gay," "queer," what sort of thing is it? A substance, a condition, a state, an attribute, an action, a logical category, or a grammatical rule? Might my naming be more like signing onto a group project? Lining up to buy a product? And what allowances do I make, *should* I make for any disagreement over names? If someone else speaks otherwise, are they wrong, badly educated, foreign, insane, or peculiar? A booklet called *Categories* has traditionally been placed first among the works of Aristotle as a gateway. Among other tasks, it undertakes to divide words by the kinds of things they name. Here is another exercise for you: Outline the *Categories* for sex/gender words in your favorite version of current U.S. English.

I now suspect that my pious hopes for the uses of "queer" were a way of relocating *queerness* in bodies, desires, and words. I do not apply "queer" as a label for a natural kind, a psychological disposition, a political allegiance, a physiological craving, or an aesthetic program—though I see how it might issue in any of those. For me, "queer" is not a name so much as a protest against complacency when naming. It records a discomfort with prevailing languages for embodiment. It is not another identity so much as a steady refusal of identification—of any settled facts of life that we are supposed (already) to know. Can one also twist "identity"? Yes, of course. Identities can be collected and catalogued as camp artifacts. They can be tried on as dazzling Nietzschean masks (see the preface to *Beyond Good and Evil* on the need for masks—and the gruesome perils of philosophical earnestness). Identities can even be accepted for a season as the least unbearable misrecognition (to paraphrase Ari Banias paraphrasing Lauren Berlant).[7] But they are not self-evident propositions about states of affairs in the world, as they are not VIP memberships in the vanguard of world history.

No queer names without queer naming, which cannot fit easily into our usual stories. When I was trying to learn the rudiments of trans speech at a particular moment in some neighborhoods of the Bay Area, I got into the habit of asking myself, "What is the register of this speech?" I meant: What is its relation to categories in the dominant or ambient languages? But my question about register was also an effort to get at the sphere of discourse in which the new languages moved. For example, did certain trans locutions belong to science, medicine, law, courtship—or theology?

Whether in the Mission or in Oakland, I heard sex/gender language interlaced with narratives of ritual and "spirituality." You can blame this on my being a teacher of renegade varieties of Christian theology. My presence in conversations no doubt pulled them in certain directions. Still, after many hours listening, I jotted down two reminders at the top of a notebook page.

1. You cannot tell a history of queer language that is only medical and scientific or only political and legal.
2. Emerging queer languages do not foretell purely "secular" futures.

In the years since, these reminders have become my axioms (in the rich sense that Eve Kosofsky Sedgwick gives to that word).[8]

If sex/gender language can be changeable and individual, if it can move across so many keys or registers, why fret over the current dominance of literalistic phrases like "sexual identity" or "gender identity"? Surely they will be gone before you know it, as an already curling wave of new words crashes down. Maybe—and maybe not.

Two decades ago, I wrote a book about some consequences of coining a theological term, "sodomy" (Latin, *sodomia*).[9] From about 1050 CE, those syllables of theological invective reverberated through treatises, laws, sermons, confessions, trials, and the cries at executions. They continued to single out and punish criminal acts in many of these United States until a Supreme Court ruling in 2003—a ruling some plot to reverse. The term still circulates, in this country and others, officially and unofficially, sometimes with lethal force.

We are in the middle of another invention: the widespread adoption of "sexual identity" and "gender identity." There are obvious differences. Sodomy was an accusation or condemnation; sexual or gender identity is supposed to convey moral neutrality or even approbation. Again, sodomy was imposed by confessors, inquisitors, other judges (both churchly and civil), legislators, and some physicians. Sexual or gender identity—originally a diagnostic category—is now supposed to be freely adopted. Certainly it is too early to foresee all the consequences of the latest invention or to calculate how long it will last. Centuries? Another decade? We do not know, though we may suspect that social networks make it easier for a term to spread and disappear more quickly than before. Perhaps so. There is still the risk—as the history of "sodomy" shows—that some of our linguistic inventions will cage us much longer than we expect—if not with their special names, then with their assumed metaphysics of naming. (Many people now refuse to say "sodomite," but they still speak of sex/gender in ways that earlier generations invented for sodomites.) The risk is greatest when a coinage fits neatly into the schemes of prevailing powers. If the modern soul has molded bodies for efficient control, so have sex/gender identities.

In the poem "Codicil," Derek Walcott writes, "To change your language you must change your life." Sometimes, at least, the reverse is true. You must improvise another language to open a way for changed life, especially if that life has been both punished and silenced.

Our lives need speech that is more adequate and evocative than the terminology of identity. That is not an exhortation to dust off antiques. I urge renewed efforts at invention. My complaint against identity-names is that they are not new enough. They are flat, boring, unimaginative, pseudoscientific, and overbearing. They barely begin to call up the artful possibilities of naming, perhaps because they disdain them in favor of "the actual facts of real life" as sciences or social groups "know them." Identity-names are not even very clever politically. They mimic the diction of the clinical-managerial terms that they are supposed to correct. A literally minded system of classification was erected to cure, confine, or discard us. Our best response is—*another* system of classification?

Does that mean that identity-words for sex/gender are irredeemable? Of course not. I would be quite content to keep identity-words if we could hear them always as a teasing joke or camp anachronism, one set of retro phrases among dozens of others. (Try listening to those the words as you would to a jukebox playing "Who'll Stop the Rain" by Credence Clearwater Revival—also very popular in 1970.) But before we can hear sexual identities differently, we have to denaturalize them. In this book, I do that in three ways. First, I invite you to reperform a selection of alternate languages—some from before the invention of sexual identity, others more recent (Chapters 1, 4–7). The alternative languages are mostly variants of English, since that is the language I use and study most. (My rhetorical method is language specific. So, I believe, is most of "queer theory.") Second, I trace a partial genealogy for "sexual identity" and allied phrases (Chapters 2–3). The genealogy shows that there was richly queer life before sex/gender identity and suggests that it should continue. Third, and throughout, I press on one of the most troubling implications of common uses for sex/gender identity: the confidence that we can give complete or even adequate accounts of human desire without noticing what exceeds our categories. For much of queer history, including the most recent, "spirituality" has been a name for that excess—for the ways to name it but also for exercises that prepare us for entering it.

I go no further in mapping the book's topics, because one of my repeated lessons is that language—especially sexual language—does not admit of clean divisions, bright-line borders, or tidy chronologies. The book hops from time to time, from discipline to discipline, from words to bodies and back. I reflect on this up front with the help of two cautionary tales ("Linguistic Orientations"), then reinforce the admonitions with an "Interlude." I lay out the main chapters as a single path through some archives of linguistic improvisations. (Hear that tension: archive of improvisations.) There are many other paths—and many ways to wander from them.

I do not use archival material for the sake of restoring some lost language. I hope rather to shift our expectations for the present and future. We have no reason to expect that sex/gender words are going to settle down any time soon. We should wonder whether we want their *permanence*. The most beautiful and suggestive words—the ones that help people fashion new ways of embodied life—might be both fleeting and local. Why apply to sex/gender language idealized expectations for stability? For that matter, why apply expectations of literal-minded clarity? How many kinds of names might be useful for our attractions, our loves? Should any one of them be permitted to claim a monopoly on "the actual facts of real life, as we know them"?

Are you perhaps already dissatisfied at my failure to define some key words that I have used regularly—especially "gender" and "sex"? Consider the dissatisfaction an index of your expectations for the clarity of available knowledge about what I blur into sex/gender. I do not find "sex" or "gender" clear. What gets called "sex" can be fertility, fate, jouissance, procreation, capital, commodity, compulsion, burden, vulnerability, violence, transfiguration, instability, and—as if underneath—a mute insistence of flesh awaiting uncoerced avowals. And gender—our ways of conceiving whatever it is rise from deep in the grammars of human domination. Defining gender is often a prelude to violence.

As I quoted Wilde's play from a printed edition, I also consulted a production typescript. The typescript belonged to George Alexander, who first produced the play in 1895 at St. James's Theatre, London. He also played the role of Jack—that is, Ernest. In this typescript, he cuts later-familiar lines to speed the action. He inserts others. He annotates with detailed stage directions. The handwritten notes remind us that Wilde's text invites performance. It means to animate bodies on a stage.

Sometimes Wilde's dialogue dictates the blocking. In the first scene, Jack takes advantage of Lady Bracknell's brief absence from Algy's morning-room to declare his love for Gwendolen. She instructs him to kneel for a formal proposal. Abruptly, Lady Bracknell returns. In one of the play's most quotable lines, she commands, "Rise, sir, from this semi-recumbent posture. It is most indecorous" (492). Jack's position is obvious—though one can imagine a staging in which he kneels only to be pushed over and straddled by an ironic Gwendolen.

Wilde subtitles the play "a serious comedy for trivial people." He means the opposite: a trivial comedy for people who want to think seriously about names, loves, conventions, earnestness, and erotic destinies real or imagined. Wilde, who has done more than most to fix one current pattern for sex/gender selves, makes fun of Gwendolen and her ideals—not least because she cribs them from the better magazines and bon mots pronounced in high pulpits or exclusive drawing rooms. But he also warns "serious" people about how far romantic ideals reach. Some "indecorous" postures can get you executed—and then, according to ancient threats, tortured for all eternity.

Imitating Wilde, I pun in this book's title. "Queer callings" means *being called by your own name, being called to* (vocation), *calling for* (exhortation), and *calling as crying out*—for help, in desire, to find your kin or the invisible powers. I do not mean my punning—or my emphasis on playful improvisation—to obscure how deeply entrenched some notions of sex/gender become or how much violence they do to living bodies. If there can be no single correct language, some languages are better than others—which must mean, less torturing.

Wittgenstein in the City of Old Words

Ludwig Wittgenstein grew up after the scientific adoption of the German word *Homosexualität*, which incited our English "homosexuality." Both the German and the English were used to classify him.

Wittgenstein writes early in *Philosophical Investigations* that a language is like an ancient city. Near the city's center, there is "a crisscrossing [*Gewinkel*] of lanes and squares, old and new houses, and houses with additions from different times."[1] Reading him thoughtfully requires variations on this image.

Variation 1: Some current languages for sex/gender are like new real estate developments. The symmetrical blocks boast every convenience, including high-speed data transmission. On the rare occasions when people mention the old neighborhoods, they tend to dwell on frequent burglaries or uncollected trash. Gazing out of your new living room, you are directed to the prairies already platted for the development's next phase. You should *not* look back at the city—which is what the angels told the handful of inhabitants they rescued from a very old city called Sodom.

But what if some day you suffer an itch to revisit the old neighborhood? Perhaps you find a brittle newspaper clipping or hear a dance hit from decades back. So, you pay the exorbitant car fare to be deposited in the irrational tangle of narrow streets. You cannot quite place yourself. That block is somehow familiar, but none of the stores are. You peer through the smudged windows at sloppy displays. The products are discards pretending to be antiques. Wait! That lamp might be an ornate prototype of the more efficient model in your living room. That poster must be the vivid original of the blurred reprint that hangs above your bed. You are embarrassed by how much you have forgotten or never knew. You moved to the suburbs but carted so much untagged baggage with you.

The persistence of an unacknowledged past is much more complicated than this variation on Wittgenstein's ancient city can show. Language is *not* divided into bounded neighborhoods. Nor is our speech about sex/gender like a pristine archeological site in which distinct periods lie neatly stratified. Sex-talk mixes them together. New terminology, even when it dominates, rarely expels all older terms. So "homosexuality" (c. 1870 in German) can be used alongside another new term with a different origin, like "Uranism" (c. 1864) or "inversion" (c. 1870), and both of them coexist with much older terms, like "sodomy" (c. 1050 in Latin) or "buggery" (perhaps thirteenth century in French).

One other complication: We do not carry old words in our hands or on our backs. We carry them invisibly—until we start to perform them once again.

Variation 2. "Our language is like an ancient city." We rarely inhabit only one language. An old city contains quarters or neighborhoods for distinct languages because set apart for certain ethnic groups. The newest, the poorest arrivals—immigrants, refugees—are still assigned to abandoned parts of the "inner city." They are compelled to learn new languages, but they also import their own. The resulting combinations can shock or delight.

However settled we are in our mother tongue, however dominant it is along our daily round, we are required to learn other languages, not least in school. For some, the requirement specifies the elite languages we call "dead." Wittgenstein opens *Philosophical Investigations* by quoting Augustine's *Confessions* in Latin. (He assumes that anyone reading him will either construe Latin or know how to find the crutch of a close translation.) The passage from Augustine claims to recall how the future saint learned to speak when he was an infant. The account assumes, Wittgenstein emphasizes, that infants acquire language by correlating things in the world with the local sounds attached to them. As if a baby said to itself, "I need milk. How *do* they articulate that urgency in this neighborhood?" In fact, Augustine describes something else—and Wittgenstein is mostly criticizing his younger self. But it is worth noticing that both begin investigating language from a scene motivated by a physical desire.

If only we could see more clearly that sex/gender languages also begin in "using the sound of the voice to show the soul's passion when *seeking, having, rejecting, or fleeing things*" (Augustine, *Confessions* 1.8, emphasis added). We do not learn words at first for delivering scientific reports or supplying unbiased testimony. The most important question for language learning is not: How can I name objects accurately, clearly, neutrally? Better to ask: How and when did I learn to express my desires—especially the ones not as acceptable as the need for mother's milk?

Variation 3. Cities of old words change around us. Each of us collects shards of the deposits from those flows. I have some of the coordinates for a map of where and when *I* learned to speak *our* language. (Perhaps that last phrase should read, "where and when this *I* that addresses *you* in *our* language was created by speaking.")

If Wittgenstein is famous for saying that there is no private language, he regularly invents stories to show how differently languages are acquired by individuals. The stories are little scripts. You can also read them as exercises to be performed.

It can be embarrassing to recall learning sexual languages. Ordinary English words for bodies and pleasures are suffused with childhood shames or rages. Recall the bedrooms, bathrooms, yards or gardens, schools and clinics, churches or temples, gymnasiums and playing fields, streets and alleys, parked or moving vehicles in which you first met those words. Focus, for a moment, just on the associated odors or noises. Where do those circumstances fit in dictionary definitions? How can the definitions be complete without them?

Wittgenstein's book of investigations or scrutinies is like a gentrified city block. On it, old and new structures have been joined in surprising ways before being refurbished to prevailing tastes. The *Philosophical Investigations*, published in 1953, is a posthumous assembly of several typescript sources in various stages of completion.[2] (At least two of the key typescripts have since been lost.) The structure of the whole volume should not be attributed to Wittgenstein. Neither should the sequence or final wording of many of the individual text blocks. For that matter, their author did not choose to publish these pages as an academic book. Speaking to a friend, Wittgenstein expressed the hope of circulating a mimeographed version of (some) of the remarks only to friends, with annotations of his dissatisfaction at particular portions of the draft.

The foreword to the *Investigations* we receive was written for a partial draft at one stage of rewriting. Still, it offers a striking image: "This book is really only an album." The album contains "landscape sketches" made during "long and crisscrossing [*verwickelten*] journeys." In the previous sentence, Wittgenstein describes his paths using the German idiom "*kreuz und quer*," translated as "criss-cross." *Quer* is a linguistic cousin of the English "queer," if not the parent. But focus on the album and its sketches or pictures, images (*Bilder*). Wittgenstein worries throughout about our pictures for how language works. He wants to supply others, less misleading. Of course, he sketches the pictures with words. He expects us to shift our favorite pictures for how words mean by learning his words.

Pursuing philosophy, Wittgenstein must use words to correct errors about words (ours and his), including some from his earlier book (the only one he authorized for publication). He had decided, at one point, to publish that first book alongside these investigations because "the latter could only be known in the right lighting [*Beleuchtung*] by contrast with and against the background of my older way of thinking" (*PI*, 4). He falls back on painterly analogies when he reminds readers that writing words about words takes time. (There is a before and after in his compositions.) But "the *right* lighting" further reminds us that relearning language involves correction.

Standard accounts of Wittgenstein's model for language resort to a slogan: Meaning is use. When Wittgenstein wants to show how meanings arise, he tells stories (offers pictures?) about the simplest exchanges: buying five red apples or moving slabs while building. His stories explain not only how the languages work but how they become habits, especially for children. Wittgenstein recognizes that his examples are fanciful miniatures. (According to one student, he would smile sometimes when proposing them—though he could react irritably if others laughed, because he also meant them to be taken seriously.)[3] You go to the grocer for five red apples. You want the apples. The grocer's job is to sell them. You speak up as plainly as you can to conclude the transaction efficiently.

Historically, many sex/gender language-games were played against plain speech. The hope was to determine, under severe penalties for mistakes, when it was safe to say what you wanted. Imagine going to the store to buy apples after martial law has made selling them a felony—when agents of the state masquerade as greengrocers to entrap you. Before saying "I would like five red apples," you might test how risky the request would be. Now, imagine compiling an album of exploratory gambits specific to queer life in the United States since 1950. Be sure to take account of race or ethnicity, mother tongue, and disposable income.

In the preface to *Philosophical Investigations*, Wittgenstein confesses doubts about publishing his gathered remarks. "It is not impossible that it should fall to the lot of this work, in its poverty and in the darkness of this time, to bring light into one brain or another—but, of course, it is not likely" (x). A friend remembers a stronger formulation: "[Wittgenstein] once said that he felt as though he were writing for people who would think in a quite different way, breathe a different air of life . . . for people of a different culture, as it were."⁴ It is important that Wittgenstein said this to a friend—since he often expresses frustration at writing for strangers.⁵ His expressions are ways of asking: Is it safe to talk?

Derek Jarman's *Chroma* is an elegy to color written while he was losing his sight to "the complications" of AIDS. The book is both spectrum and autobiography: It annotates a list of favorite colors with memories around them. Jarman returns to Wittgenstein's *Remarks on Color*. The references rest on deeper connections. He had earlier made a film about Wittgenstein, in which he claimed him as another gay man.

Was Wittgenstein gay? That may sound like a straightforward request for historical evidence. In fact, it begs the crucial question: What does it mean for anyone to *be gay*? Following Wittgenstein's own instructions, we could translate that question: In which scenes might we typically claim *to be gay* or assert that someone else *is gay*? If you consider that question even for two minutes, you can invent dozens of scenarios. They will carry different meanings of *being gay*. They will also reveal the limits both of your erotic experience and of your linguistic formation.

Jarman meditates on colors as a one-time student of painting, but Wittgenstein approaches them through everyday languages. For an introductory epigraph, Jarman combines two passages from Wittgenstein:

Look at your room late of an evening when colors can no longer be distinguished—and then turn on the

light and paint what you have earlier seen in the half-
darkness.—How does one compare the colors from
such an image with those in the half-dark room?

A color shines in its surroundings (as eyes only
smile in a face).[6]

A color shines like a flirtatious glance across a room. Or
like the deliberate smile of a friend holding back tears at a
hospital bedside.

Colors in a room under changing light, smiles of two
dozen kinds in hundreds of faces. Words, like colors or
smiles, only shine in a setting. They accumulate the history
of a community or the incidents of a biography. We make up
words in solitude but more often while playing with others.
Either sort of invention may be kept as a secret within a
select group. Wittgenstein again:

> Imagine a color-blind people [Volk], and there could
> easily be one. They would not have the same color-
> concepts as we do. For even assuming that they
> speak, e.g., German and so have all the German
> color-words, they would still use them differently
> than we do and would *learn* their use differently.

> Or if they have a foreign language, it would be diffi-
> cult for us to translate their color-words into ours.[7]

Because of his erotic attractions, Wittgenstein was assigned
to such a people. For them, as for the color-blind, the distinguishing characteristic might well be claimed as a gift, not a
limitation. Wittgenstein was blind to the locally prescribed
objects of romantic love because he had abnormal sight for
alternate attractions.

Imagine a people who learn to use "love" differently than
the majority. At what point does their use become foreign,
difficult or impossible to translate into the majority's lexicon? Consider the question again while assuming that the

majority's language of love had been edited, over centuries, precisely to exclude anything like what the smaller group yearns to speak.

Wittgenstein had written, in the *Tractatus*, "Whereof one cannot speak, thereof one must be silent." To which his friend Frank Ramsey added, "What we can't say we can't say, and we can't whistle it either."

Ramsey is sometimes included in lists of those presumed to be Wittgenstein's lovers. Other men on the lists are David Pinsent, Francis Skinner, and Ben Richards. If we read what Wittgenstein wrote to and about these men, we often encounter the word "love." Like a color-word, its meaning varies with your sight. You can use the word in a condolence letter to a young man's mother, then shift it in your journal's coded entries about him. Wittgenstein teaches that use gives meaning. Hear that as a comment on what meaning is not. For example, it is not an essence hidden behind sounds or letters. Again, it is not an exhaustive description of what a thing truly is. Meaning is no more than use, but the use of words happens alongside capacious silences. Human bodies do more than write and talk.

If the queer inhabitation of straight languages for love is not saying, not silence, and not whistling, it may be a voice calling out in the wilderness, vulnerable and persistent, at once eager and afraid of being heard.

I take Wittgenstein's image of the old city as one model for the structure of this book. You can read it as a travelogue of walks through old and new neighborhoods within our sex/gender languages. But do not assume that they belong to a single city—or that you know what it means for a city to be "one." Perhaps you should also recall that you may not recognize in some neighborhoods what counts as the erotic.

"Travelogue" is too simple. Your relation to the language samples that follow must be more active—or more receptive.

You are invited to examine them as languages that you might want to use. You should inhabit them in a way that allows them also to inhabit you.

You may already feel overwhelmed by the rapid sequence of my samples, questions, and suggestions. That is to be expected. Being overwhelmed is part of language learning and unlearning. It is also a more hopeful condition than being bored into certainty.

Sedgwick Inside a *Haibun*

"With Wittgenstein," Eve Kosofsky Sedgwick writes, "I have an inclination to deprecate the assignment of a very special value, mystique, or thingness to meaning and language. Many kinds of objects and events *mean*, in many heterogeneous ways and contexts."[8]

The sentence comes in an introduction to—a self-examination before—records of a writing project collected from the previous decade. The anthology receives the title *Touching Feeling*. Though the project still refuses to "become linear in structure," it is described succinctly as an exploration of "promising tools and techniques for nondualistic thought and pedagogy" (1). Described without being traced on a ready map or plotted against agreed coordinates. "I've always assumed that the most useful work of this sort is likeliest to occur near the boundary of what a writer can't figure how to say readily, never mind prescribe to others" (2). Or how *not* to say: the writer's craft in keeping silent. The writer's "wrestling" near the boundary "confounds . . . the self with the book and the world, the ends of the work with its means, and, maybe most alarmingly, intelligence with stupidity" (2). Recall the meanings of *dumb*, both stupid and without speech. Recall, too, what Sedgwick urges in another book: "It's only by being shameless about risking the obvious that we happen into the vicinity of the transformative."[9]

Most readers of English-speaking "queer theory" (to use that once evasive term) will recognize Sedgwick as a pioneer in the field (to speak as if in blurbs). Be careful here: One of *Touching Feeling*'s "cumulative stories . . . may be of a writer's decreasing sense of having a strong center of gravity in a particular intellectual field" (2). If they do not come together as a field-book, Sedgwick's pages do offer careful education. Their way of coming apart commends an educational reform. "Ideally life, loves, and ideas might then sit freely, for a while, on the palm of an open hand" (3). Life, loves, ideas—including ideas about how kinds of loving, sitting freely, might or might not lead into ways of life.

With kinds of love, of course, things and thingness get complicated. From volume 1 of Michel Foucault's *History of Sexuality*, Sedgwick wanted "some ways of understanding human desire that might be . . . structured quite differently from the heroic, 'liberatory,' inescapably dualistic righteousness of hunting down and attacking prohibition/repression in all its chameleonic guises" (10). She was disappointed by his little book. I read it otherwise, but I do share Sedgwick's hope for discourses about desire that pass over the prepositions *beneath* or *behind* (with their suggestions of hidden truths) or *before* and *after* (with their promises of revolutionary transformation) to feature another preposition. *Beside* makes room for diverse relations. It encourages "ecological or systems approaches to . . . identity and performance" (8). It draws the gaze back from impossibly altered futures to "the middle ranges of agency that offer space for effectual creativity and change" (13).

So far, I paraphrase segments of the introduction to *Touching Feeling*. The last essay in the anthology is "Pedagogy of Buddhism." Its frame is the misunderstood present and unsuspected past of Buddhist ways of teaching in the United States. Its main purpose is to recall an important pattern for learning: recognition and realization or the realization that is a recognition. The pattern is "the apparently tautological nature of the pedagogical scene itself," in which "one can apparently learn only what one already knows" (166). In Buddhist pedagogy, this backward turning is not "a paradox, nor an impasse, nor a scandal. . . . If anything, it is a deliberate and defining practice." Getting from *knowing* something to *realizing* it "can require years or lifetimes" (167).

Sedgwick juxtaposes Buddhist pedagogy with alternatives in contemporary Western philosophy or scholarship. In the West, "the hermeneutic tautology is always available as a fulcrum of delegitimization, yet never fully integrated in the practice of any disciplinary protocol" (166). Sedgwick connects this to an (uncited) Heideggerian paradox, probably the hermeneutic circle in *Being and Time* or "The Origin of the Work of Art." To add the obvious: Circular pedagogy does not appear for the first time in European philosophy with Heidegger. It is the centerpiece of Plato's *Meno*. When Meno tries to stump Socrates with a (just memorized) impasse in learning, Socrates replies with a myth of knowing as recollection. He illustrates the myth by working through a geometric demonstration with an enslaved person—a better learner than Meno. As the demonstration proceeds, Socrates calls out the stages of learning (*Meno* 84a–b, 85c–d). You begin by believing confidently that you do *know* something when you don't. Next, under questioning, you feel perplexed to discover that you are ignorant. With further questions of the right sort, you can acquire a dreamlike opinion of the truth (*doxa*). Repeated practice of the sequence of inquiry can lead to the taking up or recovering of the knowledge (*epistêmê*) somehow already in you.

If Socrates is ironic about the mythological origins of that possession, he is attached to the pedagogy.

Circular teaching is central to other Platonic dialogues. Socrates's best-known fable—the one about cave dwellers who come by stages to look at the sun—is a more detailed narrative of realization (Plato, *Republic* 506c–517c). The fable emphasizes the connections between a sequence of soul-faculties and a ladder of objects. Other Platonic versions are preoccupied with desire as both an obstacle and an indispensable motive. The preoccupation runs through every layer of Plato's *Symposium*. In that recollection of a memory of a celebrated drinking party, Socrates is finally compelled to lay aside his evasions enough to praise a god, Love (*eros*). He recalls—he evidently invents—the pedagogical scene in which an older woman once instructed him in "the things of *eros*" (*Symposium* 201d). This Diotima is a rather pompous tutor—that is, a self-caricature. After offering an origin myth for Love, she narrates the soul's education through a sequence of love objects, from beautiful bodies to the Beautiful itself. At each stage, the soul must recognize that it has misunderstood its own erotic attractions. It believes that it wants this kind of body, character, institution, field of knowledge. What it really wants is the reproduction of ever more intense beauties. We might paraphrase Diotima: The soul first enters the pedagogical paradox by misspeaking what it desires into sex/gender identities.

Sedgwick is famous—I cannot bring myself to say *was* famous—as the exponent of sex/gender languages beside or aslant the recommended dichotomies. As if to recapitulate all that academic labor, the first chapter of *Touching Feeling* reprises a dazzling, discomfiting reading of Henry James's fascinated hints at anal penetration by fisting, to use the current term of art. Sedgwick examines just as frankly her

own "queer" tendencies. She does this most explicitly in two
books that fall within the span of the writing project gathered in *Touching Feeling*. One is "a poetry book," *Fat
Art/Thin Art*; the other, "the extended, double-voiced *haibun* of *A Dialogue on Love*" (3). Neither should be counted
the simple or literal truth about Sedgwick, for whom sex/
gender truths cannot be either. The books show how Sedgwick moves from deciphering others' hedged disclosures to
constructing her own theaters of glimpses—her own pedagogy of circular paradoxes.

A *Dialogue on Love* is, to repeat, "a double-voiced *haibun*." *Haibun* is a Japanese genre that intercuts short prose
passages with poems—typically the very short poems English readers call *haiku*. Among the most famous *haibuns*
are the travel narratives of Matsuo Basho, especially his *Oku
no hosomichi*. The title, like the text, cannot be rendered
simply or compactly into English. It might be translated as
The Narrow Road to the Back Country (as the words say) or
to the Far North (where he actually went). But *oku* also
means the depths, an inner place, heart. Basho's title proposes travel as pilgrimage or pedagogy. Sedgwick learned to
name the mixed genre and to link it with Basho after the
death of James Merrill (*DL*, 193–94). She recalls discussing
with a friend one of Merrill's *haibuns*, "A Prose of Departure."[10] In that prose-and-poem, Merrill narrates a trip to
Japan almost cancelled because a friend was dying from the
complications of AIDS (which remains unnamed). The
haibun describes visits to clinics and cemeteries, the destinies of tombstones, the young dead, performances by dramatic ghosts and deathless puppets, the beauty of a kimono
that came from the earth and might soon be buried into it.
The anxiety that grips Merrill's trip is, the reader learns by
stages, already in the past. The ailing friend, Paul, is just
back from the clinic. Paul is dying. Paul is dead.

Sedgwick notes in the essay on Buddhism that the pedagogy of dying "brings means and ends into unaccustomed
relations with each other, and dramatizes how hard it can be
to assign the labels of pupil, teacher, and teaching on any
stable basis" (TF, 176). She reflects on AIDS and her own
cancer diagnosis. Still, if Sedgwick links her Dialogue on
Love to Merrill's haibun, she does not limit herself to voyages
of mourning.[11] The protagonist voices in the book are her
own and that of her therapist, who appears through case
notes. Both voices present versions of therapeutic sessions
and a few events around them. A reader of the Dialogue may
wonder how far both have been redacted, but it may be more
important to notice all the other voices that appear through
those two. The book contains the reported speech of parents, siblings, friends, colleagues; a selection of remembered
or anticipated texts; a number of epitomized dreams. The
polyphony describes therapy as a pedagogy, and it offers a
pedagogy in its own right.

A central preoccupation for Sedgwick's therapy is the
disunity or incoherence of her "sexuality." She is in many
ways the "wrong person" to have the interests and attractions
she feels (DL, 179). She can say, with more than ordinary
candor, that "queer stuff" is "at the heart of just about everything I do and love as an adult" (9). In the same moment, she
reports a "constant alertness in her writing about being or
becoming the right person to do it" (206, in case notes).
Sedgwick also attests that her own sexuality leaves her "stony
with puzzlement. I don't know what it is; neither do I know
its relation to what I am" (43). She almost concludes that "it's
been so much easier just to put other people's queer sexuality in the place of my own" (171).

That may sound like a penitential confession or a regret-
ful lament. The larger plot of Dialogue on Love—of Sedgwick's corpus—is to refuse the reductive command, Stick to

your own sexuality. Her therapy is animated and interrupted by mortality—the "AIDS emergency," the heartrending decline of intimate friends, the shortening of her own cancer prognosis. Attentively pedagogical writing enables companionship across several spaces and tenses, which are further multiplied by the prospect of reincarnation. If the felt nearness of death seems to scramble the sequence of teaching or the allocation of responsibilities for it, all pedagogy begins and ends with the fact of mortality. (We *must* learn because of how we are born, and we often teach because we hope to resist death's robbery.) Our spans of life do not always accommodate the pace of our pedagogies—especially when it comes to sex, sexuality, gender. Or our languages. Every "natural" language is a progressive pedagogy in at least two ways. Even a native speaker never finishes learning what the language can do. The language's changes tug all its speakers into new possibilities.

Toward the end of her therapy, Sedgwick mentions themes that appear in "Pedagogy of Buddhism." She says, "The difficult part isn't what you need to know, but how to go about really knowing it" (*DL*, 214). In the pages just before, she has described the new pleasures of weaving. She contrasts those "tactile, nonverbal, enjoyable" explorations with the anxious self-policing of her writing (206). Imagine reporting your sexuality in a book of fabric swatches.

Since I continue to be astonished by Sedgwick's agile wrestling at the border of her writing, I take seriously the testimony that her own sexuality leaves her "stony with puzzlement." To be so puzzled that you feel like a stone—immobile, without nerves or organs, removed from speech. What if Sedgwick is describing a pedagogical stage? In Plato's *Meno*, Socrates tries several times to loosen his main interlocutor's ignorance. When the third attempt fails, Meno vents his frustration. He accuses Socrates of bewitching or drugging or entrancing him (80a). He likens Socrates to a stingray that numbs anyone who has the misfortune to encounter him. Sedgwick's stony puzzlement before her own sexuality may be the numbness that begins another pedagogy.

After all, what *kind* of knowledge is a properly mature person supposed to possess about their/her/his own sexuality? Is that knowledge like the quick recall of a phone number or email address? (Some people do rattle off their sex/gender identities as if they were reciting coordinates.) Or is having knowledge of sexuality like the familiarity with home spaces that allows you to navigate in the dark? Is it recognizing your own smell on unwashed clothes? How about "knowing" that what you want right now is two scoops of pistachio ice cream? If you believe that knowing your sexuality is accomplished by finding your sexual or gender identity, could you say what kind of pedagogy "identity" implies? You don't have to be a Victorian Platonist to wonder whether erotic attractions might be more complicated or elusive than routine "information."

For Sedgwick, coming close to knowing her sexuality requires new grips on language through writing. It also demands renunciation. "I've also had to ungrasp my hold on some truths that used to be self-evident—including the absolute privilege of the writing act itself" (*TF*, 3). She ungrasps the writing act to pick up textiles. "A texture book wouldn't need to have a first person at all, any more than weaving itself does" (*DL*, 207). To revise Wittgenstein: That of which I cannot speak, I may still touch.

PART I

Identifying Selves

PART I

1

A Quarrel of Queer Glossaries

Growing up, one of my relatives-by-a-second-marriage had trouble with the words "hot" and "cold." Well into primary school, he would frequently reverse them. His mother blamed his grandfather. Whenever the old man opened the freezer that stored bulk purchases of meat, he told the boy, "Buddy, it sure is hot in there." A joke became a definition.

We speak as we have been taught. Our upbringing endows a sound or written word with an illusion of natural meaning. Once produced, the illusion is hard to dispel. Queer writers have worked hard to disrupt the "natural" meanings affixed to English words like "queer," "sex," "love," "man" or "woman." They have succeeded, at least in some speech-groups, but their success has sometimes been ironic. Their efforts left a new set of meanings feeling just as "natural" as the old. Language is not denaturalized by a simple substitution of terms—banishing some words to enthrone others. It requires ongoing fragmentation and improvisation, an active resistance to the sedimentation unavoidable in daily use. Denaturalized speakers about sex/gender would look forward and backward—reminding themselves that they have spoken in ways now hard to recall and that they will speak in ways they cannot now predict. These speakers would cultivate the habit of wondering about words or phrases that seem completely obvious. For example, if they were to speak a version of English currently dominant in the United States, they would look closely at sex/gender "identities."

We should start further back. Imagine a language that has undergone a notable change in a highly charged vocabulary: words for feelings or desires long confined to euphemism, equivocation, condemnation, or enforced silence. The change has dictated reversals for certain words (like switching "cold" and "hot"), but it has also coined new words for public use. Indeed, advocates of the change now seek to impose the new words and meanings by insisting on their rightness (naturalness?) and by shaming older forms. The language is, of course, English: Its sex/gender glossaries have undergone significant mutations over the last 130 years or so. (Some would call these mutations "revolutions," but more on that narrative fantasy as we proceed.) Now imagine that a speaker of current English becomes curious about the discarded languages—like the Wittgensteinian figure drawn back from the suburbs to the old neighborhoods of language. Suppose further that this curiosity fixes on languages pushed to the side by the victorious changes. How might you follow that curiosity?

Consider some questions. Can you recover the skills needed for fluency in the older vocabularies? (Perhaps one of those skills was deploying multiple vocabularies for sex/gender simultaneously without privileging any one of them as comprehensively true.) Can you recover some of the feelings of familiarity that once accompanied those vocabularies? (Perhaps the change in our sex/gender language has introduced a new kind of familiarity—a more intense and singular "naturalness.") Or, if you judge yourself better off without some of the discarded languages, what do you assume about the speed with which they can be purged? In George Orwell's dystopian 1984, there is a plan to replace our English (Oldspeak) with a government-issued New-speak. The plan sets goals for full replacement over seventy or eighty years. Does that seem fast or slow?

If I am suspicious of engineered language reforms, I also doubt programs for linguistic retrieval or reanimation, in whole or in part. It is not enough to restore single words. We should also not tell histories in which a single term ("sod-omite") is replaced by a neat succession of other single terms ("homosexual," "invert," "gay"). Nor should we forget that whole clusters of words for sex/gender often define them-selves by quarreling with other clusters. Their meanings are dialectical or, better, dramatic. (Clustered words for sex/gender are contending plots for human living.) To under-stand even of a little of them requires calling up competing words, images, and ways of life. I say "calling up," but per-haps I mean glimpsing or sniffing or feeling a tingle with-out pretending to reconstitute the vanished all at once in their entireties—as if they were ever fixed enough to be entireties.

Some poems and novels offer glimpses or whiffs or tingles of older glossaries for sex/gender. (I say "glossaries" because I remember Samuel Johnson's definition of the term: "A dictionary of obscure or antiquated words." It would be more accurate to replace "dictionary" with "list.")[1] In this chapter, I read portions of poems and novels that present snippets from glossaries. The texts are grouped chronologically with-out any implication of a historical survey. ("Survey" is a handy word for measuring or mapping land, but it is a wick-edly reductive metaphor for our relations to the past.) Here is the most important restriction: I focus on the sections of old sex/gender glossaries explicitly related to "spirituality." That word's current uses are often trivial. Over the last hundred years, its sweep has been grander. It has served to express exalted aspirations and to call for the overthrow of established sciences, technologies, and bureaucracies. What is more striking, "spirituality" has regularly figured in quarrels about the most appropriate glossaries for sexes, genders, and human bodies. To appreciate any of those quarrels, begin by assuming that you do not already know what "spirituality" means for them.

Douglas: The Unnamable Love (1894)

At his first criminal trial, not many weeks after the premiere of *The Importance of Being Earnest*, Oscar Wilde was pressed to explain his enthusiasm for a poetic phrase crafted by his "friend," Alfred Douglas.[2] Wilde responded:

> "The Love that dare not speak its name" in this century is such a great affection of an elder for a younger man as there was between David and Jonathan, such as Plato made the very basis of his philosophy, and such as you find in the sonnets of Michelangelo and Shakespeare. It is that deep, spiritual affection that is as pure as it is perfect. . . . It is in this century misunderstood, so much misunderstood that it may be described as the "Love that dare not speak its name," and on account of it I am placed where I am now.[3]

Though the phrase has been used since Wilde's failed defense to name almost any queer desire, his examples refer to a specific "affection," to the "spiritual" love that underwrites a pedagogy for ennobling youthful (male) beauty. Note already the defensive work of the *spiritual*. Wilde reminds both court and audience that their canonical books tacitly

approve and sometimes exalt male-male love across genera-
tions. Declaiming his defense, Wilde actively misreads
Douglas's poem to narrate a cultural history of spiritual love.
No longer in the courtroom, the poem deserves rereading.

"Two Loves" begins when a presumptively male narrator
describes a divided garden.[4] Its boundaries contain sun-
nurtured flowers but also others "stained with moonlight,"
shaped by "Nature's willful moods." To the sun side: white
lilies, crocuses, violets, lily-like fritillaries, and "peryenche"—
presumably the French *pervenche*, periwinkle. (The poem
fondles obscure names.) To the moon side: The "curious"
flowers are unnamed because unknown. They are instead
annotated according to their impossible cultivation: A particular specimen had "drunk in the transitory tone/Of one
brief moment in a sunset." Naming them would require
language suited to life on the moon—or to the realm of
"God's glory, for never a sunrise mars the luminous air of
Heaven." Of course, "Two Loves" is a terrible poem, not
least by comparison with other works published in the early
1890s (say, Rossetti and Yeats or Dickinson and Whitman).
It is not even a very queer poem. And yet it remains both
unavoidable and interesting.

A youth appears. He looks like the god Dionysus: "His
wind-tossed hair" is "twined with flowers," his lips red as
spilled wine. He carries "a purple bunch of bursting grapes."
Oh, and "naked all was he." The Dionysian youth takes our
narrator's hand before kissing his mouth. Caresses must
pause with that gesture: There is a moralizing tableau to
present, comprising "shadows of the world" and "images
of life." The reader is about to witness a personification's
allegorical tableau within a dream-poem. Nothing attrib-
utable here.

Within the nested frames, two more youths arrive from
the south. (France? Ancient Greece?) The first sings happily

of loves between girls and boys. The second does not sing.
He sighs "with many sighs." His cheeks are "wan and white,"
and the moon-flowers that wreathe his head are "pale as lips
of death." The only lively color he carries is artificial: His
purple robe is "o'erwrought" with embroidery of a fire-
breathing snake. Our narrator feels compelled to ask for the
pale youth's name. "My name is Love," he replies between
sighs. But his sunny companion interrupts to call him
"Shame" instead. Sighing once more, the insulted sidekick
replies, "Have thy will, / I am the Love that dare not speak its
name." *Have thy will*: The stereotyped script of homoerotic
submission, of pliant surrender. Douglas's poem ends there.
Readers are left to infer, of course, that the shameful lover
represents some other attraction than the "joyous love of
comely girl and boy." Something other: a love, not unambig-
uously joyous, of comely boy for boy? Say, university crushes?
(Douglas published the poem just after leaving Oxford
without a degree.) Perhaps the lunar love of Douglas's poem
is a certain phase of youth, the walled, collegiate garden a
safe, literary space for sentimental declarations. Moon flowers will and should burn under the morning sun, their
dreams with them. Queer loves bloom to wither. That is
another frame for moving them to a safe distance.

Whatever the poem's conceits or blemishes, it calls up
devices from old quarrels about sex/gender glossaries. For
example, the poem's personifications allow the lunar lover to
declare himself by performing the abandonment of speech.
Finally shamed, he becomes the sighs of the always-nameless
not-love. "I am the Love that dare not speak its name." *I am*:
Under the rules of moral allegory, that "Love" is neither an
ordinary proper name nor a common one. If Douglas per-
sonifies with abandon, he does not propose a new terminology for ordinary eros. The sighs are remains of relinquished
words, stirred ashes of forsaken libraries. The only name

remaining is more like an effacement: Shame. It allegorizes to erase. "Sodomite" has long done something like that. It began as the allegorical name for inhabitants of a city singled out in the Hebrew Bible and, so, in Christian scriptures. According to legend, the notorious city and others around it were destroyed by an angry god—that is, God. Divine wrath was ignited by a sin of some male adults, but it consumed almost every inhabitant. Though the biblical story is notably unclear, some Jewish and Christian readers interpreted the sin as sexual. After centuries of reinterpretation, other Christian theologians coined a name for the sin: "sodomy." The name proved widely useful because it had no agreed definition. Anyone convicted of the sin (now also a crime) became a "sodomite" in a nonallegorical sense. The consequences of that naming were often ferocious. A sodomite could be stripped of legal rights, family protection, social status, and Christian calling. He (much more rarely she) could be handed over to the police for prolonged punishment or painful execution.

Oscar Wilde would soon suffer the consequences of the shift from sadistic biblical legend to current criminal code. The poem by Douglas clings—foolishly or stupidly or stubbornly—to allegories. Its personifications dissolve into colors, atmospheres, episodes. Strange loves see the world under the light of another time: the last glow of a stretching summer sunset or the magic hour when sunlight thickens to gold, orange, red; runs through the spectrum on clouds; tints air. This light softens the edges of otherwise familiar things, blurs them, estranges them, and then—for a moment— allows a glimpse of their inner lights. A specimen of the moonlit flowers had, you remember, "drunk in the transitory tone/Of one brief moment in a sunset." Blades of lunar grass, "in an hundred springs," were "exquisitely nurtured by the stars." Pause the dream for a moment before it disappears. Ask, with Douglas at his most lucid, what kind of language could be made for a love within that sort of time—for loves in what Christians call the blessing-bearing vision of eternity.

Your answer might well turn to gardens, which are supposed to be reminders of a Paradise unashamed of visible genitals. The erotics of botany was firmly established by Linnaeus, who never chanced upon a marital pun he could resist.[5] By the end of the eighteenth century, the sexualization of botanical language had become so pronounced that there were debates about whether decent women should study it.[6] More than a century later, H. L. Mencken could still joke: "The only result of the current endeavor to explain [sexual] phenomena by seeking parallels in botany is to make botany obscene."[7] I doubt that he knew how far some queer authors could go. Consider the conceits in Amy Lowell's *Pictures of a Floating World*.[8] Under an epigraph from Walt Whitman, Lowell offers some delectable poems about gardens, including "Madonna of the Evening Flowers" and "The Garden by Moonlight" (which can seem a direct engagement of Douglas's imagery). The most astonishing horticulture comes in "The Weather Cock Points South." It begins, "I put your leaves aside, / One by one." A few lines on, Lowell continues:

> White flower
> Flower of wax, of jade, of unstreaked agate;
> Flower with surfaces of ice,
> With shadows faintly crimson.
> Where in all the garden is there such a flower? . . .
> The bud is more than the calyx.
> There is nothing to equal a white bud,
> Of no colour, and of all,

Burnished by moonlight,
Thrust upon by a softly-swinging wind.

One must have a cheek of stone to read without blushing. The flowers of the moon come in more genders than Mencken imagined or Alfred Douglas described.

Bodies burnished by the moon's light, which blurs into starlight or tenderest sunlight, which is celestial and heavenly and divine. It would be easy to multiply examples of alternate worlds crafted in verse of varying quality. Easy, as well, to gather from this queer horticulture many theological blossoms—references Christian or pagan, mystical or ritual. But I am more interested in how these worlds divide loves into namable and not. I keep wondering what quarrels the boundaries around gardens are meant to settle.

My questions applies to both a presence and an absence in "Two Loves." The presence is an unexplained wall: "Beyond, abrupt a grey stone wall." In context, the "beyond" should refer to the garden of the unnamable moon flowers. But its abruptness remains unexplained. Is the wall a backdrop? A boundary? Is it the border of a garden, a villa, a cemetery? Next, I note the absence—or a singular omission in it. "Two Loves" does not use the word "spiritual." The word that Wilde emphasizes in his defense of the poem's allegory, the word that enables Wilde to link Douglas with the most elevated canonical figures, does not appear.

One conclusion would be that Wilde simply imposes his reading—affectionately or deceitfully, motivated by love or desperation. Another possibility is that something else in the poem performs the work that is usually done by terms for spirit. In Wilde's speech, the "deep, spiritual affection" between older men and young "is as pure as it is perfect": pure, presumably, because not motivated by lust; perfect, because it elevates to some higher plane—because it performs an essential education. Bracket, for an interpretive moment, skepticism about Wilde's actual relations with Douglas or the current suspicion that any intergenerational interest always signals abuse. Is there anything in "Two Loves" that authorizes a "spiritual" reading?

There are spirits in the poem, but they are not spiritual in Wilde's Platonizing sense. They are ghosts. The tableau within the dream begins with a "pale pageant that hath never an end." Pale, perhaps, because a sequence of shadows and images, as the narrator promises. But pale also because we witness a pageant of the dead. Deathly pallor is also emphasized in descriptions of the sighing, lunar lover. I've already quoted some of them. His cheeks are "wan and white like pallid lilies." His lips are not spilled red wine; they are "red like poppies," narcotic flowers of the underworld. His head is wreathed "with moon-flowers pale as lips of death." His large eyes seem to signal dying: They are "strange with wondrous brightness, staring wide with gazing." In sum, the lunar lover is morbid in both medical and Romantic senses. His body figures death, and his disposition seeks it.

We could read this as the fatal destiny of the queer. There may be something in that, though for Douglas the prospect of death is somehow desirable for a sensitive soul. More: We might see a queering of the highest love through death. "There is no end to the examples which might be quoted from the Romantic and Decadent writers on the subject of the indissoluble union of the beautiful and the sad, on the supreme beauty of that beauty which is accursed."[9] But Douglas aligns the division of two loves with other divisions: sun and moon, light and dark, robust and languid, evidently living and secretly dead. What dares not speak its name is the body already promised to death. Wilde supplies the word "spiritual," absent from the poem, to induct Douglas into his defense. Douglas may not want to be inducted. He prefers to place love in the unnamable materiality of curious bodies. Of course, the word "spiritual" already reaches out to embrace that as well. It proclaims pedagogical aspiration. It offers one pole for fundamental contrasts. It fractures systems. It quarrels with supposedly comprehensive names or explanations.

The peculiarities in Douglas's lexicon go beyond the omission of "spiritual." He performs tensions without resolving them. He aligns dualities without collapsing them. He leaves suspended a quarrelsome cluster of other terms, spoken and unspoken: spiritual, morbid, mortal, unnamable, love. His title is "Two Loves." There are always at least two.

Proust: Origins of the Men-Women (1921, in English 1928)

In 1921, two decades after Wilde's death, Marcel Proust (or his long-suffering publishers) delivered the first portion of *Sodome et Gomorrhe*. The book was to be the middle volume of Proust's *In Search of Lost Time*, that novel-series or novel-as-river. Adjusted to the more delicate ears of English speakers, the volume's 1928 translation bore the title *Cities of the Plain* (a biblical euphemism). Even Scott Moncrieff's cautious rendering couldn't conceal the subject matter of the book's first section. It is "the men-women, descendants of the inhabitants of Sodom who were spared by the fire from heaven."[10] Among Sodomites preserved only for later punishment, Proust alludes to Oscar Wilde through an unmistakable description (SG, 17).

Though I attend to texts in English, I must include Proust. There are several reasons or excuses. They do not include credible evidence of meetings or literary exchanges between

Wilde and Proust. My reasons have rather to do with the
diffuse circulation of words. Proust fancied English his second language—by affinity more than proficiency. He would
be credited with a translation of Ruskin, to be sure, but he
needed much help to produce it. Still, his passion for things
English and American is undoubted. Scott Moncrieff's labors
at translating Proust prove that the passion was returned:
Sodome et Gomorrhe was Englished quickly because some
English-speaking readers desired it. I would have been one
of them.

I am embarrassed to say, then, that my concern now is not
with Proust's characters and plots, much less his inexhaust-
ible style. It focuses on his fluent switching of sex/gender
terminologies. *Sodome et Gomorrhe* opens with a dazzling
collage of idioms for homoerotic desire.[11] Most of them are
comparisons or similes: Attractions between two men or two
women are likened to something else. The likenesses range
across kinds of things but also bodies of knowledge. Proust
aligns this desire with botany, ethnography, criminology,
mythology, race or ethnicity, and sexological taxonomy (as
each stood shortly after 1900). The field divisions are mine,
not Proust's. Proust's virtuoso performance of vocabularies
displays conceptual associations by intercut repetitions.

The dominant notions are announced by Proust's section
title, worth hearing again: "First appearance of the men-
women, descendants of those inhabitants of Sodom who
were spared by the fire from heaven" (1). "First appearance"
refers both to the architecture of the series and to recent
sciences about human beings who feel homoerotic desire.
As Proust keeps saying, they belong to an invisible city, an
unmapped homeland, a shrouded world. When they do
appear to you—in a lightning-flash of recognition, in a
coded archive of notorious history—the effect can be disconcerting. Details that you had neglected snap into a pattern.

Your reassuring assumptions dissolve. That is why Proust frames this section as a drama of unexpected voyeurism.

The young, male Narrator has found a secluded perch from which to await the return from the Riviera of a duchess and her duke—two figures of his fandom.[12] He passes the time observing the blossom of one of the duchess's rare flowers in the enclosed garden. It waits on fertilization, he imagines, by a destined insect. Suddenly he notices the preliminaries to an encounter between a baron, brother to the duchess, and a (male) tailor. After cruising each other (as we might say), they retreat to the tailor's shop. Overcome by curiosity, spurred to risk more for full revelation, the Narrator moves to an adjacent storeroom (or closet), from which he can *hear* everything (voyeurism become auditory). The study of queer language is an audiophilia. What the Narrator hears is sex between two men—apparently both consensual and pleasurable. The deed is followed by a conversation at the doorway. Their talk goes some way toward restoring the social distance between them in age, wealth, and status. They move back indoors a second time. The scene ends when the Narrator confesses that he has missed what he wanted to see—the fertilization of the rare blossom in the garden. Perhaps he has heard it.

The Narrator's "botanical" contemplation introduces a first vocabulary: a scientific version of the floral scenes already sampled. These flowers are not allegories. They are living things that depend for reproduction on specialized anatomies and ecologies. The Narrator's descriptions are technical, and his horticultural examples unusual. (Proust relied on recent manuals for both.) The Narrator introduces botanical science as one detailed *comparison*: He accepts it as true without granting it the privilege of a unique literalism. The botanical episodes show how many kinds of sex deserve to be called natural. They also emphasize its interconnected variety. The correlation of the two men's specific attractions is like nature's astonishing "stratagems [*ruses*]" for introducing flowers to their pollinators. The tailor belongs to a quasi-horticultural "sub-variety" that is directed by nature, "through a phenomenon of correspondence and of harmony," to love older men (29). If you begin to hear this as a literal claim for queer species, remember that botany is the first of many comparisons, each with its clarities or charms.

Proust's section title has already cited three other vocabularies: "men-women," "descendants," and "inhabitants of Sodom." "Men-women" is the Narrator's abbreviation for the medical or scientific theory of "inversion." The article by Carl Westphal that Foucault names (ironically) as the birth certificate for the modern homosexual had proposed the new diagnosis of "contrary sexual-feeling."[13] Westphal defined it as "an inborn reversal of the sexual feeling with consciousness of the morbidity of this manifestation." Westphal's exemplary cases were (1) a woman who grew up preferring boy's clothing and then wanted sexual relations only with women and (2) a man who compulsively cross-dressed as a woman and preferred women's daily activities—but who did not express sexual desire for men. Westphal's notion coalesced with others—from sexologists like Krafft-Ebing or Ellis, from criminologists like Lombroso—to produce the diagnosis of "inversion" and the figure of the "invert" in both French and English.[14]

In Proust, the Narrator's frequent mentions of the invert (*inverti*) acknowledge and exceed the expected diagnosis. Sometimes he calls up its notions of an incurable pathology or interchanges it with medico-legal terms like "homosexuality" and "abnormality."[15] At other times, the Narrator affirms a root gender or gender nature that will show through any attempted concealments. The Narrator suddenly recognizes the baron, whom he has known for years, as a woman:

The older man has, "unmistakably" if "fleetingly," "the features, the expression, the smile of . . . a woman!" (6, compare 16). A bit later, the Narrator imagines a bedroom scene in which a woman sees her husband or male lover as another woman. In such passages, the Narrator converts the theory of inversion from a scientific diagnosis into a metaphysics of gender.

Gender is a metaphysics but also an inheritance or genealogy (in the biological sense). The "men-women" descend from a single origin. It is easy to liken them to a people or "race," then easier still to compare them with other stigmatized races, like the Jews. This comparison recurs in Proust's first section. Sometimes it underscores the race's common interests or upbringing. Inverts are like members of a particularly selective elite: They share "an identity [*identité*] of tastes, of needs, of habits, of dangers, of apprenticeship, of knowledge of commerce, and of vocabulary [*glossaire*]" (18).[16] In this phrase, note that "identity" means only sameness. At other moments, race is diluted to citizenship. The baron and the tailor resemble two "compatriots" meeting in a foreign land—Zurich, say. They are able to exchange news of home in their own language. Only their native sky is not alpine; it is best known for fiery clouds hovering over an "Oriental" desert.

The nineteenth-century sexology that the Narrator repeats is never far from fantasies of eugenics or fears of degeneration (as on 5). Once the comparison with Jews is allowed, the elaborate imaginings of antisemitism can be transferred from the Jew to the invert—who is then renamed the Sodomite (*Sodomiste*, capitalized), another figure from Hebrew history. The Sodomite remains a citizen of his destroyed birthplace, and his persistent allegiance can lead him to imagine rebuilding it (with an explicit analogy to Zionism). Still, he descends from survivors of divine wrath.

The only survivors mentioned in Genesis 19 are Lot and his daughters. Alongside generations of theologians and preachers, the Narrator imagines other survivors who (somehow) produce an abundant progeny. "They form in every country a colony" (33). They are a shadow Israel in diaspora, the reversed image of God's people. They might threaten world domination except that any conspiracy of inverts exhausts itself in bijou civil wars of self-loathing. The Sodomite returns to his native City only under the bitter compulsion of lust.

Looking back across the juxtaposed vocabularies—from botany, sexology, race ideology, biblical polemics—one passage may stand out. It describes a moment, before mating's first dance steps, when the baron imagines himself alone in the sunny garden. His face relaxes into an underlying kindness: "These features common to a whole family took on, in M. de Charlus's face, a more spiritualized [*spiritualisée*], above all a gentler delicacy" (5). The word "spiritualized" might be read only as a fancy way of describing effeminacy. But we might also take it as a claim for an unsuspected dimension to certain ways of living sex/gender.

A claim or a testimony. Reaching the glossary's last page, the reader may conclude that it has been compiled by one who knows whereof he speaks. There are so many hints. For example, we watch the Narrator concealing or closeting himself to observe the liaison. Then he repeats that inverts hide in many ways: "A great number of them at least, in a dangerous, caressing intimacy with the men of the other race [heterosexuals] . . . [speak] of their vice as if it were not theirs" (19). They speak of it—or write.

If these pages rehearse insults to Sodomites by one of their own, then the rapid circulation of competing languages can be heard somewhat differently. It might be understood, for example, as a satire of straight insults. It might also suggest that the strong passions running through sex/gender languages tint or twist them. No literal discourse is possible—not in science or scripture, not in slang or pillow talk. Even the noises made by two men having sex are misleading: They sound like a murder—only raised an octave by moaning (11). The Narrator changes languages to end by privileging none—while he insists on secrets to be heard.

Brown: A Sentimental Education (1933)

Many books are souvenirs of forgotten languages. Fewer are memoirs of how those languages were once learned. I pull from the shelf a novel that recalls what it was like to learn sex/gender in US English during the decades between the World Wars. When it was published in 1933, *Better Angel* was attributed to "Richard Meeker."[17] That was a pseudonym, of course. The author later identified himself as Forman Brown, a famous puppeteer, who confirmed that the book was thinly concealed autobiography. I leave the pseudonym in place out of respect for how hard it is to pin down names in this novel.

In summary, the linguistic biography might go something like this. Kurt Gray is raised white in central Michigan during the first two decades of the twentieth century. (However clichéd some of its features will sound, this story is not universal. No story is.) Kurt's boyhood is marked by solitude, bookish seriousness, and trouble with gender (as we would say but he would not). He is bullied. He dislikes sports and delights in staging plays (especially when he can perform as a hidden princess). Kurt discovers masturbation early—though the novel is too discreet to name the practice outright. He tries to learn more about sex by reading the encyclopedia. At one point, Kurt gives up masturbation and frets over nocturnal emissions—until his friend reports from a doctor that the excretions are natural. Note already how many vocabularies claim this young body: fairy stories, encyclopedia entries, generalized exhortations to purity, reported medical counsels. Or note the patchwork of terminologies this growing boy has had to stitch together in the effort to narrate himself.

Once enrolled in the local university, Kurt begins a sexual relationship with another young man. He has no name for what they do together: "unprecedented, this act, and unmentionable" (BA, 60). Kurt also cannot label the feelings for his partner in sin. "The idea that he was in love with Derry never occurred to him" (62). After reading modern psychology (Brill, Freud), sexology (Ellis), and literature (Wedekind), Kurt returns to the "high idealism" he finds in the Platonic dialogues—though now with their erotic resonances fully audible. Platonic love means not celibacy but the transfiguration of desire. Kurt takes a European scholarship (with study at Fontainebleau near Paris, soon after the publication of Sodome et Gomorrhe). He comes back to the artsy circles of Manhattan. Following more heartbreak and further struggles of understanding, he becomes a teacher at a prep school outside the city. There he tries to protect the students who remind him of his younger selves.

The problem of naming runs through these episodes. Even when Kurt has decided to "come out" (as we would say), he cannot find the right words. "Identity" does not appear. When Meeker's narrative wants a high scientific term, it turns to "invert" or "homosexual." For the most part, the novel surrounds Kurt's sexual life with slang, euphemism, or significant silence. The person that Kurt is still becoming at the novel's end gets called in public "queer" (repeated derisively), "scum" or "decadent pervert," "fairy" or "pansy."[18] Talking with friends or lovers, Kurt borrows quotations from Proust or variations on the symbol of Sodom.

In hours of urgent candor, Kurt considers himself marked "deep in [his] core" by an "unavoidable and uncharted fate" (176). Uncharted: Landmarks and dangers, even cardinal points, have yet to be labeled. Kurt has been handed innumerable maps with names plucked out of glossaries that range from psychoanalysis to slang. Still, he finds that his loves require him to invent both a dialect and its conceptual geography. (Place names typically precede cartography.) He struggles to find empty spaces on the official maps; that alleged emptiness is where he hopes to live. Self-naming is precisely *not* the choice of an already tabulated identity.

The glossary closest to his life is not legal, scientific, or psychological. It is literary. Kurt had read in college Alfred Douglas's "Two Loves," but other English poets hover around him. Swinburne "had come to Kurt, at nineteen, as a revelation" (62). Later, a friend recites "the subtly poisonous lines" from Swinburne's "Dolores" as he pulls Kurt into bed (136). Having become a teacher, Kurt recalls for a suffering student a line from T. S. Eliot's "The Waste Land": "I will show you fear in a handful of dust" (203). The novel ends with a poem entitled "Herakles and the Preliminary Fleece." Discovering it in an anthology he has bought by chance, Kurt is carried back to his boyhood interest in mythology—and especially the story of Hylas. (No author is named for the poem. Perhaps it is one of Forman Brown's own.) The novel begins and ends with poetry, the most capacious language for its topic—though hardly, readers have been reminded, the most approved.

I have held back two other languages important to Kurt Gray, the religious and the spiritual. They dominate the main plot's other side, in which the story is first religious and then spiritual. Since the difference between those two words matters to the novel, let me juxtapose them for the moment without comment. Kurt's mother, who passes on a love of

beauty, also teaches Bible stories (12). When a boy who has
been bullying him dies of diphtheria, Kurt feels vengeful
relief—but then recognizes immediately that both his
mother and his Sunday School teacher would condemn the
feeling (26). Later, he hunts for sexually suggestive scriptural
passages. Finding them, he masturbates to ejaculation for
the first time. Kurt's shame over the sacrilegious sex no
doubt prepares him for a revival sponsored by his church.
The preacher describes to "the boys" and their fathers the
horrible effects of masturbation. When there is an altar call
for public repentance, "Kurt suddenly found himself on his
feet, moving towards that impelling voice, and standing,
red-faced, almost defiant" (45). For some time afterward, he
clings with sentimental devotion to the desperate wish for
bodily purity. Inevitably, he fails and falls away. By high
school graduation, Kurt has given up faith in God for music
and poetry.

A few years later, back from New York for a first Christmas
home, he scorns his childhood church in favor of a higher
spirituality. "Spirituality . . . what was it? He was conscious
of it in himself without conceit, and conscious of a lack of it
in most of these dull-eyed faces around him. Yet they were
religious and he was not." Kurt remembers a composition
teacher remarking that a Polish poet was *"un homme spirituel,"* a "spiritual" man. Kurt reflects: "That was the thing,
'spirituel.' The English never had created so exact a word for
it; though many of them, he suspected, possessed the quality
to a higher degree than the French" (90). Kurt is wrong
about the history of the word in English, but that is not
important.

Later, Kurt listens attentively as a friend describes "a
cathedral, dim with incense, trembling with music, to which
young men such as they came to worship. Some were priests
in the temple, others were urchins defiling its beauty" (112).
The description is part of an invitation for a trio of lovers to

commit themselves to becoming "a priestly trinity." The book's title suggests another theological comparison: ministering angels. Against the world's slanders, an angelic choir stands immune, separate from the "great and terribly secret society" of debauched male-male desire (168). They are angels sent down to show Sodomites a way out of the destruction of despair or self-hatred.

Respecting the novel's recourse to French, we should make no assumption about the translatability of *spirituel*. Allow the word to make room for something not regularly spoken in the author's English. How does the novel fill that room? From the snippets quoted or paraphrased, you can see that "spirituality" draws two contrasts. First, it exalts certain homoerotic desires above neighborhood Christianity—and so beyond Christian condemnations. Second, the word distinguishes some erotic desires from mere copulations—from the sordid acts of the defiling "urchins," the "great and terribly secret society," the sex markets. Both uses could be heard as compensations. Queer spirituality responds to Christian proselytism by claiming to have richer access to spirit.[19] At the same time, it sets itself apart from lusts that are (rightly?) stigmatized as filthy or bestial.

Still, the uses of the word Kurt thinks new do not stop with compensation. Kurt's growth into queer maturity requires something like spiritual exercises. He seeks a way of being queer that supplies higher meaning through ritualized practices—through *askêsis*, training. For him, the asceticism is *artistic*. The envisioned cathedral, clouded by incense, trembles with music. Music is Kurt's art, explicitly likened to divine service, a calling or vocation. However jaded we are about the religion of art, we should feel—within Kurt's story—the charge of discovering that connection. *Better Angel* relies on the persisting power of religious language to sustain a sense of queer calling that encompasses asceticism, art, and vocation.

This hortatory use of "spirituality" is hierarchical. It relativizes or subordinates competing vocabularies, including the technical terms of secular expertise. When Kurt appeals to spirituality, he reduces sexology or psychology to transitional languages. They drop to a lower or earlier stage in his ascent to self-understanding; they become a partial truth or local description. By contrast, spiritual vocabularies are best characterized not by their explicit contents but by their pedagogical claims. Sexology or psychology may free you from religious bondage, but only spirituality can teach you the meaning of queer vocation. A complete education in sentiment points beyond erotic desire or romantic love to the asceticism of new worship.

Barnes: Risking Silence (1936)

Djuna Barnes's novel *Nightwood*, published only three years after *Better Angel*, crosses several of the worlds that Kurt inhabits. It describes at length the Paris of American expatriates pursuing the arts and one another. It even culminates in rural New England. Still, Barnes's languages suppose a different ecology with other risks.

The quickest reading of *Nightwood* will find spiritual and religious references. If you begin underlining words or things ordinarily counted religious, you will mark many pages of the book, some a dozen times. Early readers thought *Nightwood* a very religious book. The eminent Catholic novelist Graham Greene praised its power while distancing himself from what he took to be its horror. "A sick *spiritual* condition may have gone [in]to this book, but it is rare in contemporary fiction to be able to trace any *spiritual* experience whatever, and the accent, I think, is sometimes that of a major poet."[20] Barnes's friend and editor, Emily Coleman, claimed that *Nightwood* was *the* religious book of the generation.[21] Stepping around such grand evaluation, I select just two passages that trace trajectories through sex/gender language of religious or spiritual words. Each passage features characters that contemporary readers would call "queer."

The *first passage* records a monologue spoken by Matthew O'Connor, a doctor who hails from the "Barbary Coast" in San Francisco (then the city's district for sex work). He may practice medicine, but he teaches and lives an intricately carnal theology. In Paris, he lives near a church that he visits regularly, and he maps the city's geography by the coordinates of other churches. His monologues are bloated by Christian references, which he uses to invert (forgive the pun) traditional doctrines and devotions. "The Bible lies the one way, but the night-gown the other."[22] When Dr. O'Connor says this, he is wearing both a woman's gown and a blonde wig. The theological landscape he inhabits lies away from the Bible but along the same axis. It too offers habitation to invisible powers and alternate scriptures.

The bewigged doctor-theologian's monologue continues— as Scholastic theology inevitably does. Having confessed his own gender inversion, the doctor first pronounces a short list of the names of God from the Hebrew Bible, then describes the public urinals of Paris as his church. In a culminating evocation, he tries to inhabit what he understands as woman's desire: It is the only language in which he can speak his heart. Names of God—anonymous public sex—the desire of women under patriarchy: The doctor suffers sexual entanglements as matters of salvation and damnation. For him, sex is a desperate search for the divine in a world where God has withdrawn and only garbled memories remain of the religious. Matthew's "sexual identity," if he had one, would be a erotic desire for *God*.

As the doctor expounds an increasingly obscene doctrine, the woman listening to him is lost in her own thoughts. Nora speaks rarely in this first passage. When she does, she makes clear that she is not listening—until the doctor comes to point of talking about two other women, Robin and Jenny, with whom Nora is trapped in a love triangle. The flood of religious words, churning, cascading, has no meaning for her. It functions as acoustic filler—much less significant than the sounds of human bodies having sex. Nora desires something beyond words. One axis against which the novel measures sex runs from speech to silence or, better, to word-lessness. On the side of speech, put the doctor's endless monologues meant to conceal the wounds he has suffered from words. On the other side, Nora's side, put the wordless-ness of animals and of God, who can speak his/her/their divine name only as a flaming riddle.

The *second passage*: Near the end of *Nightwood*, the women's love triangle dissolves. Robin leaves Jenny in New York to go upstate into Nora's country. She circles Nora's house. Sometimes she sleeps in an abandoned chapel near it. One night, Nora follows her restless dog into the wood, toward that chapel. Inside, she discovers an altar: Two can-dles burn before a Madonna. There are other candles and children's toys. Robin stands there in boy's trousers.

> Then [Robin] began to bark also, crawling after
> [Nora's dog]—barking in a fit of laughter, obscene
> and touching. The dog began to cry then, running
> with her, head-on with her head, as if to circumvent
> her; soft and slow his feet went padding. He ran this
> way and that, low down in his throat crying, and she
> grinning and crying with him; crying in shorter and
> shorter spaces, moving head to head, until she gave
> up, lying out, her hands beside her, her face turned
> and weeping; and the dog too gave up then, and lay
> down, his eyes bloodshot, his head flat along
> her knees.

> (180)

I quote at length to honor words pressing against a limit, felt or declared. In Barnes, as in so many queer writers, words must negotiate the terms of their surrender. Here, they yield to a weeping silence that culminates in exhausted recognition or, at least, temporary repose. Earlier, back in Paris, the doctor's chattering Scholasticism had ended in silent tears while he sat, remembering his dead, in an official church. Nora finds Robin in a forgotten chapel reconsecrated to other powers. A reader might say: Surely this is a suggestion about a difference between queer women and queer men. Yes, it is. What is more important, it is a queer rite powerful enough to risk the return of queer lives to silence.

The silence of homoerotic desire is an ancient image for Christians, fixed already by the founders of Latin-speaking theology. Jerome claims that the Hebrew word "Sodom" in Genesis meant "mute beast."[23] Later theologians appropriate Ephesians 5:3 for unnaming a particular sin. Having recited a list of transgressions in that passage, Paul warns his readers: You should not even talk about these things, much less do them. Later theologians used the prescribed silence to designate, by paraphrase, something too vile to say: *peccatum sine nomine, peccatum nefandum*, a sin both nameless and never to be spoken aloud.

Casting homoerotic love into bestial silence has been a familiar strategy for Christian communities. A contemporary queer writer who returns to silence risks confirming or reactivating the old violence. Might the risk sometimes become necessary? Say, as resistance to coerced labeling? As a haven for what in sex/gender resists all words?

I have pasted together a collage of glossaries, featuring four of them. This collage claims no privilege. The selected texts are not offered as canonical, best, or most beautiful. I chose them because I had been with them long enough—as a reader and teacher—to feel some confidence in hefting their languages. (A reminder to academic historians: Knowledge *about* words is not yet habituation in their meanings, which are their uses.) I could have made other collages—and I will in the pages that follow. Each time I select elements, part of my purpose is to provoke you to pick up others, more congenial to your tastes or more familiar from your past.

The collage of this chapter samples words about sex/gender. My samples are not statistical so much as musical: I borrow my use of the verb from dance music I first learned to call "house." (Its names have multiplied since, encouraged by rival fandoms.) "House" tracks are held together by an irresistible 4/4 bass beat that drives at some 120 beats per minute. Many other sounds are layered on top of the bassline, but I listen especially for the vocal "samples." These quote singers from a range of musical genres, disco to Gospel. Most striking are the familiar snippets—songs you have heard before, far from the dance club, that now soar above the beat that shakes you. Following the words produces a sense of dislocation or, at its strongest, of transgression. (Should I be dancing in a gay club to that Baptist hymn, that clip of Latin chant from Lent?) After the sample repeats and repeats, dislocation becomes an occasion for hearing the words as if for the first time.

This chapter's collage of texts on sex/gender has no organizing beat. Its rhythms are irregular, its samples not always as transcendent as the soprano flights of house. Still, the textual collages may dislocate some words to sound them anew. I count on your finding at least a few of the century-old locutions familiar—even if you were raised on the terminology of sex/gender identities. I hope that hearing them in older contexts will dislocate any assurance about their uses—say, in relation to a word like "spirituality." If you like the illustrations called word-clouds, you might imagine the collages of older texts as word-clouds in which still familiar sex/gender terms appear alongside others from quite different discourses. We have not always assumed that clinical sciences could or should assign us our truest names. We have not always acquiesced in claims that there were uniquely true names for our sex/gender.

2

Inventions of Identity

Most any collage of queer glossaries from a century back can remind us how different current names are. The changes are not just in slang or popular speech, which we expect to age quickly. More important shifts happened in basic assumptions about the relations possible between sexes, selves, and communities.

What stories should we tell ourselves about changes in English terms for sex/gender since Djuna Barnes published *Nightwood* in 1936? A story of progress? The bad old terms were replaced by good new ones, and superstitious babblings yielded to scientific clarities. Or do we want to declare that the discreet murmurs of political weakness were finally pushed aside by the forward march of a boisterous victory parade? Either of those stories raises another sort of question: Do the social and political "victories" since 1960 or 1990 prove that clinical terms converted to political labels are *truer* than the words in use before? But I get ahead of myself. The rapid rise of identity-language applied to sex/gender is a story in itself—and perhaps the story to be told before others.

Where did "sexual identity" or "gender identity" come from, and how did both spread so far, so fast?

Here is the shortest answer I can give: Our terms "sexual identity" and "gender identity" descend from efforts by some scientific authors in the 1950s to shift debates about sex/gender from biology to psychology for therapeutic purposes. Their efforts were supported by sociological studies of group formation and psychological interest in individual integration. They were amplified by the rapid spread of other kinds of "identities" across academic disciplines and public discourses after the mid-1950s. A decade later, "gender identity" and "sexual identity" had effectively if confusingly fused psychosocial meanings with minoritized politics and the expression of an inmost self.[1]

My version of the shortest answer leaves out many things. For example, the notion of a "minority identity" for "homosexuals" goes back through "homophile" movements in the early 1950s to the radical US politics of earlier decades. The notion of an "identity" as the deep self, the individual's core, has its own tangled genealogy, amplified and further confused by sociology, ethnography, psychology, and psychoanalysis before and during the 1950s. Let me emphasize: The interlaced genealogies of these words are too complicated to be summarized or even traced coherently. Still, snippets of genealogy can help orient a search for the clinical origins of "sexual identity" and "gender identity."

I start with the obvious example: Erik Erikson is often credited with popularizing the notion of identity for US readers. In one passage of an influential book from 1950, he traces the basic meaning of the term to brief remarks addressed by Freud to a Jewish association. Freud's 1926 letter includes what Erikson calls an "untranslatable turn of phrase" that "contains what we try to formulate in the term 'identity.'"[2] The phrase, as Erikson quotes it, is "*Heimlichkeit der gleichen inneren Konstruktion.*" He renders it as "the secret familiarity of identical psychological construction" (CS, 241). This must be reckoned an overtranslation—not to say, an interesting misquotation. The word that Erikson translates as "identical" (*gleichen*) has no etymological relation to the German *Identität*. For the *Standard Edition* of Freud in English, James Strachey renders *gleichen* as "common": "the safe privacy of a common mental construction."[3] What is more interesting, Erikson misquotes Freud's German, substituting *inneren*, "inner," for *seelischen*, "mental" or even (in a religious context) "spiritual." Taken together, the overtranslation and the misquotation suggest that Erikson wants to invest the passage with more significance than it can bear. When Freud testifies in the previous clause to "a clear consciousness of inner *Identität*," he refers to nothing more definite than a feeling of likeness with other Jewish members of the association. He does not claim to possess an identity; he recalls that he was consoled thirty years before by an inarticulate familiarity. It is Erikson who wants Freud's recollection to ground a theory about identity as the connection between individual and group. Freud means "identity" as felt sameness; Erikson wants it to be something more usable.

Addressing the members of B'nai B'rith, Freud acknowledged that he was never linked to the group by religious faith or national pride. His consciousness of shared sameness had to do with freedom from intellectual prejudices and a willingness to live without the majority's approval. Freud does attribute the two dispositions to his "Jewish nature" (*meiner jüdischen Natur*) and to his being "a Jew" (*weil ich Jude war*). With these ordinary expressions, he points to the ways that shared upbringing can foster easy friendship. He also—quite deliberately—gestures toward the violent ideologies of nineteenth-century racial "science." (We have already heard some of them in Proust.) Freud's "untranslatable" mention of identity is a racialized simile. According to ideologues, to be a Jew in Vienna during the 1890s—even a secular, not particularly Zionist Jew—was like belonging to an alien race. Since antisemitism is much older than Erikson's identity-language, it is not clear which linguistic frame should be regarded as larger. Is being Jewish an *example* of having an identity or is it a (racialized) *prototype* for the very notion of group or personal identity? Proust puts similar questions about being a sodomite.

For the moment, I stay with Erikson's eagerness to find some anchor-hold in Freud for the language about identity he means to advocate—even if the hold is a few sentences in a brief and still recent cover letter. Overtranslated and mis-remembered, unsettled by racial allusions, the passage is asked to secure the astonishing range of "identity" in Erikson's *Childhood and Society*. The passage is cited about two-thirds of the way into the book, but the keyword has been used from the second page of the foreword. *Childhood and Society* introduces itself as "a psychoanalytic book on the relation of the ego to society" (12). It has just defined the ego as "the core of the individual" and reported psychoanalysts' current concern with "the ego's roots in social organization" (11). Hear the sedimented analogy in "roots": The individual ego grows from and always depends on surrounding society. In (many or all) "tribes and cultures," childhood is the period for growing a "particular form of mature human *identity*," a "unique version of *integrity*" (12, emphasis added). The pattern for an individual's core varies by culture. So must the social steps for making a core that will ground or contain the ethical resonance of "integrity."

Erikson is interested in plotting the stages of "the life cycle" from birth to maturity, but he insists on leaving space for future investigation. (The insistence becomes stronger in the second edition.) He also attends to historical shifts at the largest scale. His interpretation of Freud's remarks to B'nai

B'rith supports an argument that the study of identity in the United States after World War II is as "strategic" as the study of sexuality was in Freud's Vienna. Identity replaces sexuality as the psychoanalytic lens for entire cultures. Just here, Erikson underscores the newness of his uses of "identity: "We begin to conceptualize matters of identity at the very time in history when they become a problem. For we do so in a country which attempts to make a super-identity out of all the identities imported by its constituent immigrants"— including Erikson himself (242). *Childhood and Society* mentions "sexual identity" once; it seems to mean the sense of being female or male (228). A few pages later, describing a "utopia of genitality" with "lasting social significance," the book remains resolutely heterosexual (230–31). A sexual partner (please, one at a time) must not only be "loved" but "of the other sex" (and there are only two).

The book's swirl of identities can dizzy a reader. In an essay published a few years later, Erikson confesses to a little dizziness of his own. "I can attempt to make the subject matter of identity more explicit only by approaching it from a variety of angles—biographic, pathographic, and theoretical; and by letting the term identity *speak for itself* in a number of connotations."[4] When it speaks to Erikson, "identity" often refers to individual configurations but also to continuity in personal character, ego synthesis, and solidarity with group ideals. Identity speaks itself through identities that are individual and shared, distinctive and cross-cultural, synthesized and continuous. I add: Identity is depth psychology and shared destiny, ethics and politics—almost (if we recall the word) theology.

You will understand, then, why I long ago tightened my focus to "sexual identity" and closely related terms. They are dizzying enough. I mean to represent just a few of their gyrations, looking beyond to slower drifts of words for sexed selves. As Wittgenstein explained, as the last chapter's collage of literary texts illustrated, old words persist alongside new ones. Terms disappear only to reappear with other meanings, and the discarded linguistic past solicits us whenever we open its books. Something was "new" about the emergence of sex/gender identities in US speech during the 1950s, but the change did not bring about revolutionary purity or an abolition of all prior memory. (To speak more cautiously: It has not yet succeeded in doing so.) A plausible story about these new uses for "identity" is more likely to be parodic than monumental, dissociative than antiquarian, self-undoing than bombastically critical.[5]

Scientific Glossaries for Sexual Identity

Let me pick up gyrations near the middle. In a paper from 1959, a psychologist, Thomas Colley, proposes to define "total sexual identity" by drawing together earlier authorities.[6] Indeed, Colley boasts that his notion will combine biological, sociological, and psychological insights. It can retain what is true in Freud's account of psychosexual development while taking on the more recent discoveries of cultural anthropology (Margaret Mead), the neo-Freudians (Fromm, Horney), and interpersonal psychologists (Rogers, Kelly, Sullivan). Erikson is cited only later, as an object of criticism (NO, 175n6). But Erikson's project pervades this essay. Colley wants "total sexual identity" to serve as what Erikson called a super-identity, an identity that absorbs and takes over the functions of other identities. Colley counts his contribution as a theoretical explanation, but it might be better understood as a linguistic manifesto.

"*Total* sexual identity" coordinates multiple technical terminologies under a psychologist's ideal of a stable self. Coordination is a salient function of Colley's definition.

Adult sexual identity is supposed to be, first, a *biological* fulfillment of the "natural" development that makes one male or female. Next, *sociological* sexual identity reflects a society's particular specifications of maleness and female- ness in dress, behavior, and dispositions. Then, *psychologi- cal* sexual identity includes "characteristic ways of perceiving one's sexual interactions with others who are identified as being of the same or opposite sexual identity" (167). Total sexual identity combines these three spheres while allowing them to vary independently if sometimes inappropriately. Here is another important function of Col- ley's definition: the conceptual separation of supposedly discrete elements—or, at least, elements that he claims can be measured separately.

The relation of sexual identity to maleness and female- ness is more confusing. Colley's opening paragraph reads: "Persons do not exist; there are only male persons and female persons. . . . There is no human identity uncomplicated by sexual identity." He then steps back: "Personality evolves as either masculine or feminine, or as some combination of the two" (165). If sexual identity complicates human identity, it is complicated in turn by the statistically recorded combina- tions of its elements. Describing psychological sexual iden- tity, for example, Colley not only isolates it conceptually from biological and social forces, he separates an individual's relations to members of the same sex from relations to mem- bers of the other. Note to the contemporary reader: You may feel the impulse to rewrite what you have just read using the word "gender." Stop yourself. "Gender" does not figure in this article.

Colley supplies an origin story for the individual's total sexual identity. The "sexual paradigm of nature" decrees that an individual should have a "prosexual" (attractive) response to persons of the other sex and an "antisexual" (aggressive) response to those of the same sex. "To the degree that there is lack of disturbance of the [paradigmatic] expectations . . . there will be appropriate [psychological] sexual identity" (170–71). Note the backward construction: Appropriate identity results from *lack* of disturbance. A child acquires appropriate expectations by learning from social interactions, especially with parents. "The parent 'projects' [psychological] sexual identity into the child" (172). Wittingly or unwittingly, the parent also passes on deficiencies of identity. But Colley is careful to distinguish his theory of identity from accounts of imitative *identification*. Familial or group identifications only partly explain the building up of an identity. I would add: Identification by imitation cannot perform the functions that Colley wants to assign to total sexual identity.

Pause over the last point. It is tempting to understand gender and (then) sexual *identity* as simple extensions of psychological or social notions of *identification*. Connections are indeed obvious. But definitions like Colley's claim more than imitation can explain. The proposed consolidation of psychotherapeutic, sociological, and anthropological identities demands other causes and processes. It also places the whole sequence under the master category of identity rather than identification: The result sounds more like a thing than an activity. For Colley, as for Erikson, an identity is accomplished as a stage of development. It is something you *must* do to become appropriately mature. Crucially for later uses, a sexual identity can also be posited while admitting that its underlying origin is unknown. Alongside the coordination of technical terminologies and the distinction of independent elements, securing confidence in the predictive power of identity despite agnosticism about causes is a third function of Colley's proposed definition. You can use a sexual identity for therapeutic management (or social

engineering) without having to explain its specific causes—
ever. I would call it a *deus ex machina*, but it is not a god that
appears.

Note as well an ambiguity in the effort to enumerate the
functions of Colley's definition. The ambiguity is connected
to a larger doubling of perspective that has been with us
from the juxtaposition of Wittgenstein and Sedgwick. When
we talk about the "use" of a word, we may have in mind its
grammatical or logical functions within sentences. But we
may also mean its appropriations into the applications or
arrangements of power. If Colley defines "total sexual identity" in order to resolve certain theoretical problems, he
recommends it for its clinical advantages: "The present
approach may provide for earlier and more accurate diagnosis of disturbance in psychomodal sexual identity" (176).
More: Colley's total sexual identity is expected to intervene
in the quarrel of experts over who gets to name sex. I can
make this clearer by juxtaposing another author whom Colley does not name.

Written for Harvard's interdisciplinary program of "Social
Relations," John Money's 1952 dissertation treats the balance
of physiological and psychological causes in various kinds of
people classed as "hermaphrodites." The dissertation argues
that people can indeed adapt themselves to the "sex of their
rearing" whatever is happening physiologically. It also shows
that the various kinds of people who have been classed as
hermaphrodites are able to "make an adequate adjustment
to the demands of life."[7] Within the dissertation, Money
gives the term "psychosexual orientation" both narrow and
broad senses. The narrow sense refers to "individual erotic
preferences—the direction and goal toward which libido is
exercised" (I-281). In the broad sense, "sexual orientation"
(Money's shortened term) also includes "outlook and
demeanor" or "outlook and deportment" (I-288, I-190). Money

makes a strong claim about both senses: "It appears that psychosexual orientation bears a very strong relationship to teaching and the lessons of experience and should be conceived as a psychological phenomenon" (I-202). Money's rejection of a purely biological or physiological account of orientation emphasizes that causal explanations are embedded in disciplinary terminologies. Kinds of causes correspond to spheres of expert speech.

Money will make new expert speech before the reader's eyes. In the dissertation, he acknowledges that the proper meaning of "gender" is grammatical (see his note, I-36). Over the next few years, he transfers the word, very deliberately, to name the new clinical possibility opened by the malleability of "outlook and deportment" in relation to sexual difference.[8] By 1955, Money and his new coauthors begin to write of "*gender* role" in a capacious sense.[9] The phrase is interesting in three respects: for using a still new sense of "gender," for asserting that gender is a "role," and for continuing to include the erotic or sexual *within* gender. In his first monograph after the dissertation, Money reverts to speaking of "gender role and erotic orientation."[10]

The redeployment of the old word "gender" is worth yet another pause. In Kurt Weill's 1943 musical *One Touch of Venus*, the goddess, on a visit to earth, complains: "If gender is just a term in grammar, / How can I ever find my way, / Since I'm a stranger here myself"? Money is not writing witty lyrics for Broadway. He is making language for new therapies of sex/gender. The transfer of a grammatical term into the clinic—or the operating room—authorizes practices. It may also transfer expectations. For example, if we expect grammatical gender to follow rules of consistency, comprehensiveness, and so on, do we now expect that of "gender identity"? If English has a notoriously limited system of grammatical gender, do we expect "gender identity" to abide within those limits or to compensate for them?

Money's stuttering change of terms did not elicit immediate agreement from his peers. Other psychologists continued to speak of "sex role" and "sex role identification." They would do so for decades. Still, across his texts, Money moves toward a threefold division that foreshadows common usage. The division comprises *bodily sex* (with all its levels and ambiguities), *gender role* (both social and psychological), and *erotic orientation*. When Money stresses that gender is largely learned rather than innate, he means once again to stress its "psychological" origins. Yet his emphasis on learned gender—not to say, his own disciplinary placement—allies him with those who understand gender as the *social* expression of anatomical or biological sex. Already in the 1920s, academic authors begin to speak of "social sex adjustment."[11] By the 1930s and 1940s, their terminology proliferates into "social sex adjustment," "psycho-social sex aberrations," "social-sex development," and (simply) "social sex." In all such phrases, "sex" refers to what Money begins by naming "psychosexual orientation" and then comes to call "gender role."

The proliferation of terms shows the confusions attending the birth of categories amid equally plausible alternatives. It draws attention to authorial choice. Colley chooses "sexual identity" as the master term, while Money selects "sexual orientation" and then "gender identity." Underneath the master terms, both authors separate out independent components while insisting that they remain congruent or coherent. Both also try to mitigate some of the paradoxes of nature and nurture. But their concepts remain unclear even as the new terms spread. Neither Colley nor Money wants to waste time on the quandaries underneath the emerging terminology—quandaries arising from binaries like mature/

immature, adjusted/maladjusted, functional/dysfunctional, treatable and not. Their strategy is to break off pieces from physiological models to defend a separate clinical space. The defense will be ongoing—and it will move from the clinic to the streets, from therapy to activist politics.

There is another confusion here that has been overwritten by our habits for distinguishing gender from sexuality and narrating the history of trans persons as distinct from the history of homosexuals (when in fact the two histories are inseparable). In the 1950s, as in the late nineteenth century, analyses of homosexuality often rest on models of switched gender. We have seen a sample of this persistent discourse in Proust. Many other examples lie near at hand. They show that for the early sexologists we credit with inventing the category, homosexuality is not just inseparable from trans-sexuality (to use our terms) but dependent on notions of gender reversal. You can recognize something similar in the 1950s and 1960s: "Sexual identity" depends on "gender identity," terminologically and conceptually.

Making Identities Manifest

Reading Colley and Money, I do not pretend to have sketched a "complete history" of gender/sex identities in the 1950s. (Histories cannot be complete: Clean-cut segments are not to be found in the flow of human time.) I am also not trying to tell an *in*complete history, if by that you mean an account of the most representative or important figures or events. (Historical importance is less a feature of the world than an ingredient for satisfying stories.) I only hope to illustrate, from two limited examples, the rhetorical gravities that pull on mid-century names for sex/gender. My selection of examples has to be even stricter for the 1960s. It is tempting to move at once to the decade's end, when "sexual identity"

becomes a central term for the manifestos of emerging
social and political movements. I add first only a few reminders of how complicated the circulation of the new terms
was—and remains.

In the background of the manifestos, technical terminologies coined in the 1950s gained ever more popularity. For
example, books familiar in homophile circles (as they were
still known) claim that being a homosexual is an "identity"
or "sexual identity."[12] In *Stigma* (1963), more compellingly,
the sociologist Erving Goffman describes "personal identity" as the "single record of *social* facts" that becomes the
"sticky substance to which still other biographical facts can
be attached." Among the stigmas of character traits, Goffman lists those "inferred from a known record" of homosexuality. He uses homosexuality throughout the book as an
instance of "spoiled identity."[13] Of course, Goffman then
subordinates the meaning of "identity" to his elegant vocabulary for describing roles and performances. Equally important was the circulation of the complementary technical
notion "gender identity." In the early 1960s, specialists in
intersex conditions speak of "gender role and identity."[14] By
1964 at least, this becomes the idea of "core gender identity."[15] In 1966, a "Gender Identity Clinic" opened at John
Hopkins Hospital, the existence of which was acknowledged
a year later on the front page of the *New York Times*.[16] The
specific labels are less important for future speech about sex/
gender than the reiteration of "identity." It affirms that there
is a thing to be achieved or induced so that it can be possessed. You *have* sex/gender identities.

The disentangling of "sexual identity" from "gender identity" was accelerated by feminist critiques of supposedly
natural femininity. The activist manifestos that proliferate
at the end of 1960s put "sexual identity" into much wider

circulation. Let me illustrate from a single manifesto, *The Woman Identified Woman* (1970).

> As the source of self-hate and the lack of *real self* are rooted in our *male-given identity*, we must create a new sense of self. . . . Only women can give to each other a new sense of self. That *identity* we have to develop with reference to ourselves, and not in relation to men. . . . Together we must find, reinforce, and validate our *authentic selves*. . . . With that *real self*, with that *consciousness*, we begin a revolution to end the imposition of all *coercive identifications*, and to achieve maximum autonomy in human expression.[17] (emphasis added)

The notion that a created or discovered identity expresses the real self might seem an uncanny echo of "clear-cut core gender identity" in Stoller. Stoller's "identity" means to describe the ways a person "unquestioningly feels that he or she is a member of the assigned sex," a "solid" conviction that can be "shattered" only at enormous psychological risk.[18] Stoller also supposes that such an identity deserves free expression in various ways. But this simply applies to gender what Erikson had said about ego identity, about the core of the self. Remember, too, that settled personal identity requires for Erikson a sense of being a woman or a man. It is no surprise that manifestos written in the late 1960s or early 1970s assert the urgency of expressing an inner sex/gender self within a community that shares the effort.

A manifesto is an emphatic act of public speaking. "Coming out" looks like a spatial metaphor but it refers to prescribed ways of saying one's self to the public. The real or "authentic" self, validated in group consciousness-raising, is called to be much more than a private conviction. Its declaration contributes to repairing the world. This self lives for and in the future. (Coming out is performed in a sort of future tense.) Temporal projection aggravates the obvious tension in a revolutionary movement's demand to come out. On the one hand, coming out is the declaration of your true self, which you have so far kept hidden. On the other hand, your declaration drafts you into a struggle to produce a future self through a transformed society. Conceiving homosexuals or inverts as a political minority goes back in US speech at least to the early 1950s. By the 1960s, the claim has been rewritten: Being a member of a persecuted minority confers group identity.[19] At the end of the decade, that claim is increasingly fused (or confused) with the individual expression of deepest selfhood. *Our* identity as a sexual minority becomes *my* sexual identity as a person. So far, so Eriksonian. But if "coming out" is in some sense a political prophecy, it is also the longing for an eschatological self—Shakespeare's Miranda marveling at a "brave new world," the only fit stage for "goodly creatures."[20] New identities for a new world.

Despite the fervent rhetoric of *The Woman Identified Woman* and hundreds of other manifestos, the revolution never arrived—not even in speech. A politics based on claims of identity was not received with universal acclamation even within "lesbian/feminist" and "gay male" groups. Already in the mid-1970s, there are complaints against it in the underground press.[21] There are also attempts to reinterpret both coming out and gay identity as processes of integration into a larger sense of self.[22] Before the end of the decade, the criticisms would be louder. In short, a lot was being written already in the '70s about the dangers of thinking one's true sexual being through an identity—especially one countersigned by the state.[23] If some astute thinkers also criticized these criticisms as a form of gay erasure, they too wished for something more than stable identity.[24] On the other hand, none of this writing seems to have slowed the spread of identity-language for both sexuality and gender, now too neatly separated. If revolution has not yet dawned, there have been palpable—habitable—linguistic shifts. Of course, the spread of "sexual identity" far outruns liberationist efforts, and it reinforces the confusing associations with other meanings after being picked up for political use. (Remember Colley: "Sexual identity" is a label able to coordinate if not devour other labels.)

A single example supports both points. In September 1970, *Harper's* published a sordid essay by Joseph Epstein with the subtitle "The Struggle for Sexual Identity."[25] Reaction was swift. The newly organized Gay Activist Alliance submitted a set of four replies to the magazine.[26] All were rejected. In response, the GAA staged a "zap": Forty members occupied the magazine's offices for a day. There was a heated exchange with the editor, Midge Decter, who then disappeared for lunch. At the close of the action, the occupiers left voluntarily with a sense of success. I mention this episode for the language around it. Despite its subtitle, Epstein's essay does not use the phrase "sexual identity." He quotes or appropriates variations on derogatory words for male homosexuals: pervert, fag, roaring fag, tough fag, queer, closet queer, latent queer, and so on. He calls homosexuals furtive, desperate, flamboyant, freaky, swishy. While he pastes many names on homosexuals, Epstein does not assign them a specific sexual identity. The nearest he approaches is to say that homosexuality has become, tyrannically, "a full-time matter, a human status" (50). So, was the subtitle for the published essay Epstein's? Or Midge Decter's? And what after all does the key phrase in it mean?

The cover, which pictures Epstein's essay, shows a muscled man in a sparkling, "feminine" shirt. The essay is illustrated with photographs of effeminate models or manikins. For the editors or designers, gay sexual identity is the confused presentation as male and female. (Interestingly, this is how *Harper's* had used the term around 1950—before it was redefined in clinical settings.)[27] Within a few months of the zap at the magazine, one of the organizers—Merle Miller—published a reply to Epstein. He wonders whether the shaky "sexual identity" of a particular heterosexual classmate led the man to be grossly rude at a high school reunion. Miller then assumes without comment that there is a range of sexual identifications across human beings.[28] With that, the new meaning slips in unannounced—and from an accomplished journalist rather than a drafter of manifestos.

The political activities of the Gay Activist Alliance and many similar groups point to other networks through which the new term spread: the US legal system. In the first half of the 1970s, "sexual identity" still means in US courtrooms what is now called "gender identity."[29] But the notion of "sexual orientation" was gaining ground as a rough synonym for the new, activist meaning of "sexual identity." In 1973, for example, the District of Columbia banned discrimination on the basis of "sexual orientation" by any employer. This language was retained when the District issued a comprehensive Human Rights Act in 1977. Beginning with an executive order by the governor of Pennsylvania in 1975, regulation or legislation of different scope was promulgated in many jurisdictions at an accelerating rate. Some of these texts were then amended or supplemented to include "gender identity." Although "sexual orientation" remains the more frequent legal term for several decades, by the 1990s "sexual identity" makes regular appearances in law review articles and the first specialized casebooks.[30]

The legal propagation of notions about sexual and gender identity highlights a deep assumption in *The Woman*

Identified Woman and hundreds of other activist documents: Claiming identities is necessary to social progress in the United States. There is no way to gain political traction without them. Doubts about identities are rebuffed—often angrily—with the charge that taking them away would remove the only political basis for hard-won rights. I am not convinced. When we tell recent LGBT history in the United States, we often substitute "gay liberation" for larger, slower movements around sex/gender issues. I have heard students, colleagues, and other friends repeat as self-evident that "the movement" began with the Stonewall street demonstrations towards the end of June, 1969. That is wrong. Even within the (provincial) purview of the United States, the start date is off by at least two decades. (Proust's narrator has already suggested that European efforts began in the nineteenth century. Indeed, the German original behind "homosexuality" was conceived for one of those legal efforts.) But the mistake is not just in dating. The claim that significant political progress only became possible with the rhetoric of "gay liberation" is, at very least, debatable. Though I doubt that large-scale historical causality can be proved one way or the other, I am ready to argue that significant change in the United States may owe more to the methods of the Mattachine Society than the Gay Liberation Front. For that matter, it may owe more to novelists, dramatists, and poets writing from the late nineteenth century on.

Perhaps you are thinking: But what about the widely reported *feeling* of having an identity? Are we not obliged to honor so many sincere testimonies? I tread carefully here. Just over my shoulder there are whole histories of violent naming. In English, as in most European languages, many sex and gender names were coined in religious condemnation, moved to criminal accusation, and then translated into medical or psychiatric diagnosis. The linguistic history is a sequence of coercions and punishments—which are, of course, often declared to be (spiritual or physical) cures: "We stigmatize you for your own good." Who can blame the bearers of such blood-soaked names for rising up to demand the right to rename themselves?

I do not blame them. I join them in lament and resistance. But I still want to allow the old Socratic questions: What do you mean when you say that you "experience having an identity"? Might there be more helpful ways to articulate a persistent sense of self or its relation to surrounding societies? Does sharing have to make us the same?

I have told you a bare story about the clinical origins of "sexual identity" and "gender identity," then outlined another for their public circulation after 1970. There are longer and more detailed stories to be told. I expect that many of them would converge around my plot points: Our identity-terms for sex/gender were coined to serve the applications of new sciences. They projected categories or entities through promises of clinical management. Social analysis, political activism, and legal reform then borrowed the terms for other urgencies and realized them by other means. Whether they convince you or not, my stories ought to raise questions about my purposes. What do genealogies of words offer, and to whom? What do they accomplish in narrating shifts of language from archival selections? After all, a "history of sexuality" can also be animated by a vaguely therapeutic faith that insight into conceptual origins will cure readers of something. Or it may hope to neutralize the harms of inherited teachings by deciphering the plans and plots behind them. Still, meditating on the purposes and limits of genealogies, I return to Wittgenstein's picture of the old neighborhood and to Sedgwick's polyphonic confession. Genealogy leads us back through our learning of languages. It opens decisions we had closed. It estranges our mother tongue(s). In sum, genealogy may help us handle language less thoughtlessly. It might even make space for learning it otherwise.

Which discipline gets to conduct linguistic genealogy? Foucault is not alone in claiming it for something called "philosophy." Socrates made himself obnoxious by asking people to define terms they brandished daily. He was not just collecting definitions. He pursued them to interrupt the famous fluency of Athenians. Then and now, people imagine that they know what their words mean. They take pride in owning their language. This is fantasy. We can perform acts of linguistic meaning, and we do hold our languages intimately. But they also hold us. "Knowing what I mean" and "knowing English" are phrases illustrating that verb's confusing breadth. What kinds of knowledge can we gain about how we talk now?

Consider a specific version of that question: How do we talk about sex/gender now? You might rather start by asking, Who is the "we" and when is the "now"? English has never been one language, and none of its versions has kept still for long. In the preface to the Herculean *Dictionary of the English Language*, Samuel Johnson warns that words in wide use "are hourly shifting their relations, and can no more be ascertained in a dictionary, than a grove, in the agitation of a storm, can be accurately delineated from its picture in the water."[1] A dictionary that seeks to reflect current usage reaches just as far as its "corpus," its archive or database of examples. A corpus is a corpse: It consists of remains. The evidence for a dictionary memorializes the compilers' decisions about geography, chronology, and genre or kind. The evidence is subject to hazards of recording or preservation—not to say transcription, since samples of speech must be written down. More: Efforts to *make sense* of a linguistic corpus—say, to organize its examples into definitions—require interpretation, imagination, and applications of taste. Johnson is candid about his own tastes and their limits. A similar candor should be expected for the taste that bills itself as "objectivity."

All of this becomes more vexed around sex/gender. Unless you believe that sexes and genders really are the definite creatures of clinics or courtrooms, you will sense from familiar examples how far they roam beyond standardized speech. Imagine that someone lent you an immense database containing global uses of "sex" and "gender" during the last twenty-four hours in (what you could recognize as) English. How would you begin to interpret it? How could you verify that you had understood each of the samples? Johnson: "When the nature of things is unknown, or the notion unsettled and indefinite, and various in various minds, the words . . . will be ambiguous and perplexed" (*D*, preface [v]). And when would you want samples from the next twenty-four hours? Nothing is more stylish than slang—which means, nothing boasts more local expertise or contends more volubly over correctness.

My amateurish and perhaps too philosophical study of sex/gender language convinces me to abandon schemes for comprehensive certainty. Better to start, as Socrates did, with what is near at hand, seeking simpler insights into how some (not "we") have talked recently (not "now") about sex/gender in an English that I might inhabit at least part way. I offer a few written exercises in different ways of knowing some of the sex/gender usage around me. Each exercise is supplied with its necessary prologue.

Exercise: Gathering Samples Near at Hand

Over the last five decades, I have taught in US colleges and universities. Dozens of such schools have recently published booklets to help their members understand one another better and offend one another less when talking about sex/gender. I endorse those goals enthusiastically. But I also notice that the efforts to prescribe speech often repeat the confusions of expert discourses since 1955.

A first example: A 2020 booklet from a unit at Harvard University defines gender identity as "one's internal sense of being male, female, neither, both, or another gender. *Everyone has a gender identity*."[2] Is the phrase I have emphasized an empirical claim (everyone reports having this sense), an ethical prescription (everyone should have it), or a grammatical rule (every speaker of English is assumed to have it)? What if someone reports *not* having that internal sense? Or what if they are just unwilling to play the sex/gender language games on offer? Perhaps they are to be told, "Unless you accept these assumptions, you cannot join our conversations."

Here's a second example. In the headnote to a section entitled "Sexual and Romantic Identities," a *Common Language Guide* prepared for Amherst College warns: "Identity terms mean very particular things to different individuals. . . . The best way to truly understand what an identity term means is to ask someone who uses that term to name their own sexual identity."[3] Good advice, not least because it recognizes that sex/gender speech is local and changeable. Still, the *Guide* assumes that every member of the college (at least) will be able to "name their own sexual identity." How exactly is asking them to "name" supposed to give you *true understanding* of what they mean? Note one other thing. Amherst's *Guide* defines some 230 words or phrases, but not "identity." Dictionary definitions for basic terms are often circular: They must suppose that a reader accepts some words in order to explain others. It is important, even so, to observe where defining stops. The assumption seems to be: Everyone knows what identity means. Quite the opposite, in fact. After decades of listening to classroom discussions and reading student papers, I regard the most intense sex/gender speech as an idiolect, an *individual* assembly of language fragments, often baffling to speakers and hearers alike.

I regret singling out these two, good-hearted pamphlets. They do not deserve special criticism. Word-circles like theirs appear in uncountably many efforts to sort current talk about sex/gender. The notion that it can be sorted or settled is no doubt part of the problem. To return to Johnson: "Sounds are too volatile and subtle for legal restraints; to enchain syllables, and to lash the wind, are equally the undertakings of pride, unwilling to measure its desires by its strength" ([viii]). Measuring desires might also be like lashing winds.

Exercise 1. Imagine that you are assigned to lead a discussion with a group of strangers about some topic touching on sex/gender. Write out any rules of conduct that you plan to propose at the start of the conversation. Now try to sort them into two columns, one labeled "Manners or Ethics," the other "Language." If you succeed in sorting them, describe the rule or sense that you rely on. If you cannot, describe your incapacity. If no rules occur to you, write a quick script for the words or gestures you will use to start the discussion.

Exercise: Composing Wittgensteinian Dialogues

Faced with the omnipresence and elusiveness of supposedly *ordinary* language, Wittgenstein resorts to schematic

dialogues. They outline language games for beginners—
for young children learning language, for older children
attempting philosophy. My second exercise takes off from
a simple-sounding question: For which basic language
games is "sexual identity" indispensable?

Start a step back with the always confusing shift from
"identical" to "identity." Gore Vidal liked to complain that
"homosexual" was an adjective for acts rather than persons.
He refused to use the word as a noun or to "come out" into
any other nounlike label.[4] A similar complaint might be
lodged against imposing an identity wherever you describe
some things as identical. Put this into a Wittgensteinian
format.

> A goes into a shop to buy one red apple.

> The shop owner, B, places two of them on the
> counter. "Which of these would you like?"

> A says, "I can't decide. They look identical."

> B picks up one of them. "Why not take this?"

> A nods. "That's fine. It still carries its identity."

> B laughs. "There's no extra charge for that."

*Side thought: Perhaps there is a hidden charge for slipping
from a characteristic of human relations to a species-attribute
in human individuals. Maybe we have been paying the sur-
charge for some decades now.*

Shift now to a schematic sex/gender conversation for
another sort of transaction.

> A stands a little awkwardly at the edge of a social
> meeting for those seeking something other than
> "straight" dating. The meeting is about to end.

> *B*, a very attractive stranger, approaches *A* with a broad smile. *B* says, "Ready to go home? How about with me?"
>
> *A* smiles back. "I would like that. But I need to ask you one question first. What is your sexual identity?"
>
> Puzzled but still smiling, B replies, "Do I need one to get into bed with you?"

Your first reaction may mirror mine: The dialogue is completely unrealistic. It omits essential details of flirtation: gestures or "body language," costume, tone of voice or kind of laugh, eye play, fragrance. The format of Wittgenstein's didactic language games does not fit erotic exchanges. That suggests a larger challenge in representing erotic encounter. Even the much richer descriptive capacities in Sedgwick's *Dialogues on Love* fall short of convincing flirtation—they resemble more the disconcerting abstractions of Roland Barthes's *A Lover's Discourse* or Monique Wittig's *The Lesbian Body*. Of course, once you set your mind to inventing dialogues you can imagine seductive uses for an apparently out-of-place question about sexual identity. In specific contexts, for example, it might be posed to inquire flirtatiously about genital configuration, sexual tastes, dating history, or commitment to queer politics. For that matter, almost any sex/gender classification can be used ironically, comically, teasingly, or salaciously for erotic ends. If you have doubts on this score, review the titles, blurbs, and typical dialogues of pulp novels from the 1950s.

Let me rephrase the question motivating this exercise. For what kind of exchange can you imagine using a question about "sexual identity" in some nonironic, nonflirtatious way?

Suppose I were at a doctor's office . . . There the question would be a polite way of asking what kind of sexual acts I engage in to assess the health risks they might pose.

I could be answering questions from the police . . . If I were in a jurisdiction where same-sex acts were legal, my "sexual identity" would be sought in connection with other facts known about an incident or suspect.

I could be at a political rally . . . Then the question would be a way of estimating the degree of my commitment.

I could be filling out an official form . . . But *what is* the function of "sexual identity" as a contextless piece of information about me—unless it is to confirm me in believing that I possess such an identity and must do my best to safeguard it?

Exercise 2. Imagine that you are asked to write Wittgensteinian dialogues for teaching current meanings of "sexual identity" or "gender identity" to an extraplanetary alien untutored in human reproduction. Would what you have to teach before you could begin to explain identities? How much of your explanation would concern reproduction? You may suspect that these questions wonder whether "gender identity" must be taught before "sexual identity." But they also wonder how far these identities are trapped by a 1950s metaphysics of the social as against the biological.

Exercise: Listing Uses (Counts for Triple Credit)

Pretend that I do want, after all, to summarize for myself current uses of "sexual identity" that I have encountered. Since the term is a fairly recent arrival in general English, I decide to focus on the advantages that are supposed to derive from adopting it. What does a sexual identity promise to do for us? I emphasize sexual identity because this exercise has to be done differently for gender identities in the context of prevailing medical power.

When Wittgenstein analyzes ordinary language, he relies partly on his own experience of speaking, partly on what he hears others saying, partly on what he can imagine as typical. In the same way, my evidence for what I am about to say comes from places I have lived during certain years, but mostly from classes taught, debates joined, books read, blogs visited. My habits of using or interpreting sex/gender terms are shaped by my race, my level of education, my friends, and my tastes—to name obvious limitations. But this kind of particularity seems to me appropriate for thinking philosophically about our actual uses of language. After excusing his errors and shortcomings, Johnson writes that he collected uncatalogued words "by fortuitous and unguided excursions into books, and gleaned as industry should find, or chance should offer [them], in the boundless chaos of living speech" ([iii]).

In the boundless chaos of current US usage as I hear and repeat it, a sexual identity has at least four functions. If you agree to put it on, it will comfort you, instruct you, organize you, and market you.

(1) Sexual identities *comfort*. They simplify what is confusing, domesticate what is wild. They make stable sense out of the flux of desires, feelings, memories, sensations, acts, partners, or scenes. Sexual identities also supply ready language for what can otherwise leave us tongue-tied. Belonging to something like a natural kind offers a solid connection with others who share in it. Identities can assure you that you know what you are.

(2) Next, sexual identities *instruct*. They set shared expectations about how to behave, what to like, what to wear when, and whom to admire.[5] A sexual identity promises a complete style, a distinctive and comprehensive *persona*.

Since identity-instructions can be quite specific and quickly outdated, part of the pleasure of sporting an identity is keeping up with its fashions. It is interesting to contrast (2) with (1). Does a species have fashions?

(3) Sexual identities *organize*. They can count off unitlike members of a political group. They dial down individual differences in service of solidarity. They also supply the pivot on which social stigma turns into an affirmable essence. "Dyke!" or "Faggot!" becomes "Lesbian separatist" or "proud Gay." The reversal can be a momentous step, both politically and psychologically. Of course, the artificial unity of the reversed insult may supply only a cruel solidarity. Its promise of organization relies on the false claim that all those once stigmatized by the insult were really alike after all. Contrast (3) with (2). Does the play of style sit well beside the earnestness of movement politics? Is that earnestness best understood as monotonous style?

(4) Last but hardly least, sexual identities support markets by fixing descriptions for quick exchange. In olden days, the printed personal ads of *The Advocate* abbreviated sexual preferences with symbols based on widespread slang. An upright classical column indicated "Greek top," while a column on its side meant "Greek bottom."[6] (Note to any befuddled reader: A "Greek top" prefers to penetrate the anus of a "Greek bottom.") The charms of rustic simplicity! Now there are many more precise categories for describing sexual products on sale. Even simple "dating" apps offer a drop-down menu of finely differentiated brands.

I stop with four functions of sexual identity. The short list should illustrate some unexpected effects of adopting identity-terms. It may also recall some of their unintended consequences, now increasingly obvious. For example, and as we all know, sexual identities tend to multiply endlessly. Since there are no agreed criteria for how much of what kind of difference counts as a *new* identity, we make more of them—as many as people want, until there are so many that they are hard to use with any certainty. The old "handkerchief code" popular in some gay bars required one to distinguish lavender from fuchsia at 1:45 AM under dim lighting. (A mistake would mean that you were volunteering to be spanked when you were actually seeking a drag queen who could share your enthusiasm for Dolly Parton.) The current menu is much more unwieldy. A recent effort to list sexualities omits fetishes and derogatory terms to reduce the number to eighty or so.[7] Another recent list of genders runs to some 360, each with a flag.[8] I love lists and enjoy inventing words. (I am not so interested in lining up behind flags.) So, I would gladly receive these and other tabulations as delightful products of "the exuberance of signification" or even "lust of innovation" (*D*, preface, [vi], [iv]). That would mean, of course, resisting demands to regard the identity-terms literally as either ethical orthodoxy or political imperative. For some of us, the multiplication of sex/gender identities is also worrisome because it resembles so many other market processes, like branding or fandom. For others, becoming a brand or gathering fans is an aspiration.

If sexual identities seem to fulfill certain promises before defaulting on them, it is also important to notice what they never pretend to promise. A socially legible sexual *identity* cannot encourage incommunicable fluidity, unpredictable mutability, free improvisation, or wild invention. A sexual identity will gradually carry more of an official past than an unexpected future. It will reflect the prevailing common sense, which is so often the repository of power's achieved results. Most of all, a sexual identity will be burdened with the ambient plots, the approved stories of encounter or relationship. Any deep transformation of the sex/gender order requires a more persistent breaking and remaking of words than identities register or predict.[9] That transformation can include—indeed, may perhaps best begin by—rambunctious play within identity-language. But that play may already concede too much—namely, that the most serious names for sex/gender are likely to combine the authority of some science with the political experience of an organized community. However familiar, the scientific-political genealogy may be false. It may also be dangerous.

Exercise 3. After such a long introduction, please feel free to make your own list of some salient functions carried out by identity-terms for sex/gender. You may run on as long as you like. Once you stop, scan the completed list. How would you now undo it? Would it be enough to add examples of contradictions or unintended consequences? Perhaps a more illuminating list would begin from some version of the question, what do you want sex/gender names to do? And how do you already conceive their functions in advance? For example, your desires might assume that such names should only describe, approve, guide, or lure. What if they also bless?

Exercise: Sex Names and Sex Shame

The queer glossaries of Chapter 1 showed something of the range of comparisons for human sexuality. The last century's sex/gender labels depended on analogies to natural species (including insects and flowers), ethnicity or race, hereditary degeneration, local or national citizenship, socioeconomic status, level of formal education, degree of artistic sensibility, and so on. The glossaries also connected sex/gender names to religious histories and mystical spiritualities. This is hard for us to remember. The loudly secular character of prominent US movements for sexual liberation can imply that being lesbian, gay, trans is the opposite of being religious—or, at least, that supposedly scientific terms like "sexual identity" or "gender identity" must be exempt from the violent histories of religious shames. But examples in last two chapters have suggested that medical shames might be at least as powerful as religious ones. When medicine took over the management of human sexuality from religion (I speak schematically), it may also have received the main economy of shameful naming.

What explicit or implicit *affects* run through sex/gender identities? Consider two kinds of names. The first are familiar insults against those who live erotic lives against the paradigm of compulsory heterosexuality: "queer," "dyke," "fag," "bull-dagger," "*maricón*," "sissy," and so on. Over recent decades, some people stigmatized by these terms have tried to reverse the negative charge into something positive. Now consider a second kind of name. These are scientific or medical names supposed to be both precise and neutral. "Homosexual" is the obvious example, but I would also include some older names ("invert," "homophile") and some names for whole classes of names ("sexual identity," "gender identity"). While it is acknowledged that many of these names have dubious genealogies, it is often assumed that their origins can be stripped away to reveal the precise, neutral core of meaning. But are the affective auras around the words really just a soft husk?

Even when removed from their original programs, clinical words carry the force of a diagnosis. They also and easily acquire new charges of social shame. The apparent neutrality of the clinical terms encourages their rapid appropriation into new programs of condemnation. "Gender ideology" is now the code word by which many "conservative" groups dismiss changes in social attitudes toward sex/gender. They support their condemnations by appealing to allegedly scientific evidence from medicine, psychology, and sociology. Their traditionalism is, of course, thoroughly modern: It embraces a rational positivism with which it then deforms older religious teachings. But the easy absorption of new medical and scientific terminologies for sex/gender into traditionalist condemnations must count against any confidence that clinical terminology can provide guarantees against shame.

Another question lurks here. It has to do with the ways a sex/gender identity packages sexual feelings and experiences, including shame. If you are ashamed, the packaging says, it must be because of your identity. A single text can help undo this curious claim. In 1980, Michelle Cliff published a book entitled *Claiming an Identity They Taught Me to Despise*.[10] The book is a sort of *haibun*—to import that genre word once again. Cliff assembles prose and poetry to explore the complications of "identity" across race, religion, geography, familial memory, bodily surface. The section from which the book takes its title narrates her search for a sense of self through memories of racial insult and grading by skin color, of passing, of domestic violence and its ambient fear. It shows that "identity" refers in fact to a more or less habitable self put together despite a legacy of insoluble conflicts and secrets still mostly unsayable. "They" in Cliff's title are legion, and what they teach you to despise is so much more than the abstract idea of an identity. When you are ashamed of being queer, you are typically not just ashamed of sexual desires or gender assignment. Shame also squeezes how you talk or sing, how you walk or gesture, how your skin smells or gives off heat, how your body looks—the very fact that you live as a body. Conclusion: If what they teach you to despise is so much more individual and embodied than an identity, you cannot rid yourself of shame by reclaiming or redefining an identity.

Exercise 4. Recall Susan Sontag's cautionary remark at the beginning of her controversial essay on camp: "A sensibility (as distinct from an idea) is one of the hardest things to talk about but there are special reasons why Camp, in particular, has never been discussed. . . . To talk about Camp is therefore to betray it."[11] Is talking about your sex/gender as an identity inevitably a betrayal? Discuss.

Exercise: Identities and the Factories of Power

During decades, my reading has followed a hunch: Treating any significant human feature as a *thing* (species, complex, essence, allegorical personification, -ism . . .) renders it more available for manipulation by power. You can also turn that formulation around: Networks of power make the *things* they need. Not a few contemporary projects of sexual liberation have assumed that they could repurpose the things made for the networks of power that they meant to overthrow. Take a term useful in classifying persons (say, sexual identity), remove any religious stigma or clinical odor, and then redeploy it with a smile. I simplify, but not by much. Do we really think power is so easy to nullify? Or that it is so stupid? If you can reverse the charge, the polarity, of a term by political declaration, you can also re-reverse it. Indeed, by amping up the reification or personification in certain categories (like "queer"), you can make them newly useful to prevailing power.

Exercise 5. Suppose you foresee that any new words you use for sex/gender will be quickly appropriated into the violent discourses of religious or political zealots. How might you design language to resist attempts at exploiting it for persecution, prosecution, or "therapy"? Will you begin with particular words or the sensibilities elicited around them? Will you design booby-traps or prescribe regular exorcisms?

3

Identities at Prayer

The association of sexual inversion with ritual religiosity was, in Victorian or Edwardian England, as notorious as the link between perversion and criminality or degeneration. It was obvious enough to be the object of frequent satire.[1] The association was also durable: If you credit Evelyn Waugh's account of Oxford in 1923, advice to an arriving undergraduate included this stark warning: "Beware of Anglo-Catholics—they are all sodomites with unpleasant accents."[2]

A more considered view of sexual character and religion is presented by Havelock Ellis in *Sexual Inversion*, published in 1897 from his own work and that of his deceased correspondent, John Addington Symonds.[3] Paraphrasing Féré and Raffalovich, Ellis concludes that though the invert "may not have in him the making of *l'homme moyen sensuel* [the average red-blooded man], he may have in him the making of a saint" (147). Ellis notes the erotic condition's prevalence among religious leaders. More interesting than the correlation is its interpretation as evidence for a special spiritual capacity with ethical and political benefits. Ellis receives this view partly from Symonds, who begins A *Problem in Greek Ethics* with the claim that the Greeks not only tolerated "homosexual passions" but deemed them "of spiritual value."[4] Ellis himself paraphrases an argument from a pamphlet whose author he does not mention: "The special value [of same-sex love] lies in its capacity of being exalted to a higher and more spiritual level of affectionate comradeship, so fulfilling a beneficent social function" (35). The pamphlet is by Edward Carpenter.[5] In the discussion of "homogenic love," as in other writings over decades, Carpenter analyzes the "spiritual side" of same-sex love to show at once its necessary physical manifestations, its social utility, and its capacity for personal transformation.

Later chapters will say more about queer spiritualities. For the moment I point to this older teaching because it still found receptive readers among US activists in the 1950s and 1960s. It served as a tattered backdrop for ongoing discussions of sexuality and religion—specifically, homoerotic love and Christianity. It was against this backdrop that new questions were posed, loudly and urgently, beginning around 1970. How were Christian theology's old powers for refashioning language to be deployed when the new sex/gender identities appeared in general circulation? Christian or not, you live amid the responses.

Early Borrowings

Even from the last chapter's simplified genealogy, you might judge "sexual identity" an unpromising candidate for use by Christian theologians. You would be right—and wrong. The term made a quick transit from medical and sociological uses into political activism that was decidedly hostile to Christian churches.[6] Then it jumped even more quickly from activist manifestos to "progressive" Christian writers.

And then—here is a significant surprise—it was put to opposite uses by writers vehemently opposed to sexual liberation in general and to gay pride in very particular. Perhaps this reversal in the use of identity-language will be more plausible if we step back quickly, and as before, into the 1950s.

From the mid-1950s on, Christian theologians writing English were drawn into debates about the criminal prosecution of same-sex acts between consenting adults. Once engaged, they began to reconsider church policy. An Anglican theologian, Sherwin Bailey, is the eminent example— and not only because his work figured in both British and US debates over decriminalization. In April 1952, Bailey proposed an Anglican study group on homosexuality. Two years later, the new group issued a preliminary report, *The Problem of Homosexuality*. The report advocated decriminalizing same-sex activity in private between consenting adults on grounds of justice and new psychological knowledge. The next year, Bailey published his own monograph, *Homosexuality and the Western Christian Tradition* (1955). The book argued that church history both tutored and confused contemporary attitudes about same-sex desire, especially between men. He concluded that the errors and deficiencies in church condemnations of male-male love deprived current criminal law on homosexuality of any supposedly Christian justification.

Bailey's historical arguments would go on to influence church deliberations, political campaigns, and university-based scholarship. He put them to more immediate uses. Acting as a private scholar, he submitted a historical monograph to the "Wolfenden committee," that is, the (British) Departmental Committee on Homosexual Offences and Prostitution (appointed in 1954 by the home secretary). Bailey also edited the final submission to the committee by the Church of England's Moral Welfare Council.[7] In the next year, the Wolfenden committee endorsed decriminalization. A decade later, parliament passed a Sexual Offences Act that accepted the Wolfenden committee's main recommendations and so endorsed much of Bailey's reasoning. By then, Bailey's pioneering books had been joined by a number of other Christian arguments for a new view of sex.

The history of this change in the views of some Christians is interesting. It deserves to be better known. Still, I keep my focus on the basic categories that these authors did or did not use. The category "sexual identity" does not appear in Bailey's 1956 monograph. It is not used by Robert Wood in *Christ and the Homosexual* (1960). It is not mentioned by dozens of respondents to the survey conducted in 1964 by the (San Francisco) Council on Religion and the Homosexual.[8] When the word "identity" does appear in the 1967 edition of Norman Pittenger's *Time for Consent*, it has only the sense of identical or equal.[9] (Pittenger speaks of erotic attractions as "sexual orientation.") There are a few technical references to deviant identity or gender identity in Oberholtzer's *Is Gay Good?* (1971) but no systematic development.[10] And so on. It is difficult to prove a word's absence in an uneven textual archive, and it is boring to try. My conclusion is still that "sexual identity" gains traction in Christian writing only in the early 1970s—after the notoriety of manifestos like *The Woman Identified Woman*. The category crossed from activist manifestos into theological writing through individual biographies. Here are some examples.

On November 11, 1970 (the month after the *Harper's* "zap"), more than four hundred students and faculty from local seminaries gathered at the Pacific School of Religion, atop its glorious hill in Berkeley, for a public panel on homosexuality and Christianity. The preacher at the day's liturgy was Nicholas Benton, who took as his title "Was Jesus Homosexual?" Benton had spent much of that year writing pieces that were soon published as a pamphlet, *God and My Gay Soul*. His language evolves rapidly even from piece to piece. So too does his understanding of the proper relation between revolutionary analysis and Christian theology. Benton often mixes identity language with other phrases, but it becomes increasingly important for him.

Benton wants a theological notion of gay identity to match what he hears in the "movement"—to reproduce the fused meanings already in circulation (psychological and sociological, personal and political). But Benton adds meanings of his own, wittingly or unwittingly. He first distinguishes "gay" as personal discovery from "homosexuality" and "homosexual" as labels of oppression. For Benton, the homosexual is analogous to the *male*-identified woman in allowing "her or his self-identity and life to be governed by the straight man's value system." The gay, by contrast, "is involved in the process of discovering a 'gay' self-identity and life style." Again, "'gay' is the person, identity and life style."[11]

Since a sexual identity *is* the very person, it acquires rights of free self-expression. It then expands with the horizons of self-discovery. The "perspective" of "the new self-affirming homosexual consciousness" is "totally different." It requires a revaluation of all (heterosexual) claims and the creation of a new culture—together with a new theology or spirituality. The *soul* has a new identity (as Benton's title proclaims). Its liberation should lead to freeing "the World Gay Soul" (10). "Symbolically perfect" rituals of oral sex in ever-expanding groups might overcome even the barriers of gender: "A total community of all persons of the human race participating in total mutual affection can be actually experienced" (11).

Benton is eccentric—not least in his direct transfer of prescribed polyamory from revolutionary manifestos into Christian proclamation. If his eschatological visions do not gain wide acceptance, his shift of terminology foreshadows changes elsewhere. In 1972, the Methodist youth magazine, *Motive*, after breaking from the denomination over sexual questions, spent its remaining funds to publish twin issues, a "Lesbian/Feminist Issue" and then (the very last) "Gay Men's Liberation." The language of identity appears often in these pages but without Benton's mystical prescriptions for global group sex. According to one author, for example, a woman-identified woman stands up to male definitions by saying "I define myself," so expressing a sexual preference that is a politics.[12] One of the editors of the male volume found his "gay identity after a year of closeted, dishonest bisexuality." Both editors of the men's issue commit themselves to "an understanding and obliteration of this masculine power identity [as] we continue to form our analysis and to seek our identity."[13] The last issue's other pieces obliterate more dramatically: "I cannot think of a stronger means of confronting America than by helping others to stand in front of it and say, *together*: 'I am Gay; I am Proud, and you will deal with my existence.'"[14]

Here is another early example of movement language crossing over into churches. In 1973 (three years after Benton's sermon), a number of academic institutions in and around Atlanta hosted a conference on "theology and body." The pastor of a local congregation, John W. Gill, spoke under the title "The Gay Identity Movement." He explains: "This is not a liberating movement. It's not a movement of revolution. It's an evolution of identity within the homophile community."[15] His explanation rejects the (vernacular Marxist) rhetoric of revolutionary liberation while retaining its claim that an identity is first of all an obligation to speak. "We homosexual men and woman are not just listening anymore, we're starting to speak out!" For anyone attuned to Christian genres, Gill's speaking out

sounds less like a liberationist manifesto than a testimony—
and not in the legal sense. Testimony is an evangelical
genre in which self-narration builds a church. Gill uses it
for telling his conversion to an identity. In other publications, Ralph Blair explains: "Your homosexual self is a part
of you,—the you God loves. You are free to be his most
faithful son or daughter within your very own sexual identity. He does not ask us to give up our sexual identities."[16]
Indeed, you praise God by testifying to them. Interestingly,
Blair's dissertation on homosexuality from a year earlier
does not refer to "sexual identity" in its text or in the survey
questions on which it relies.[17] This suggests, again, that
identity-language enters progressive church language very
quickly in the early 1970s.

A final example, to confirm the timing. In a 1974 volume
coedited by Sally Gearhart and William Johnson, the language of identity appears unevenly—and not quite where
one might expect. Johnson's own piece sets out from "the
collective life of every oppressed minority" but then shifts
quickly to Paul Tillich's call for courage in the "essential"
affirmation of one's "own being."[18] Johnson speaks throughout of "sexual orientation," which he defines as "the *primary*
emotional, psychological, erotic and social responsiveness
experienced by human beings" (*LW*, 105). Gearhart's contribution, an expanded version of her widely read manifesto,
does speak of identity but only in relation to the woman-
identified woman (e.g., *LW*, 130, 139). It is the academic
theologian—Robert Treese—who adopts the language of
identity without qualification (e.g., *LW*, 40, 45, 46). What is
more striking, Treese imposes the terminology on the New
Testament when he revises the paper for inclusion in the
1974 anthology.[19] To repeat: Between the mid-1960s and the
early 1970s, Treese moves the notion of sexual identity from

his paraphrase of psychologists and sociologists to his theological assessment of Christian scriptures.

Unexpected Confirmations

In these and dozens of other texts from the early 1970s, we can catch not just the crossing over of sexual identity into Christian texts but a growing ease in its use—a spreading sense that it has been the topic all along (even for passages in the New Testament). If Benton combines identity-language with visions of global sex, other Christian writers domesticate it. They connect it to familiar authorities or use it as the obvious vocabulary for self-description or count on it as the necessary idiom of progressive politics.

The absorption was contested by Christian authors of various ethical and political views. Some criticize any effort to reduce human being to sexual identity.[20] Others, including advocates for a change in church teaching, reject it as too culturally driven to be theologically useful. Consider John McNeill's influential *The Church and the Homosexual*. First published in 1976 but drafted several years earlier, the book speaks frequently of the "sexual-identity image": "Every culture has created its ideal sexual-identity images for the masculine or feminine role."[21] These (gender?) images include dispositions of sexual desire, such as heterosexuality. But McNeill does not endorse identities or their images as adequate; he calls on theologians to criticize them. Homosexuality is "an organic challenge within society to the partial and dehumanizing aspects of these sexual-identity images" (134). McNeill also explicitly rejects any claim that such an image should be confused with the self: "The essential point I have tried to establish in stressing the positive characteristics of homosexuality is that the tendency to identify oneself as a person with one's sexual-identity image can, and frequently does, lead to a one-sided stress on certain qualities and the elimination of others" (149).

If you can find theologians on various sides of the new terminology, how did it finally take hold in Christian speech? The archives suggest at least two answers. The first is a progressive accommodation in denominational statements on sexuality right through the 1970s. The second, more interesting, comes nearer the end of the decade and points in the opposite direction.

Denominational statements issued during the 1970s show a bewildering range of terms and much confusion about their meanings. The confusion is made worse by the bad habit of citing biblical texts or ecclesiastical law to condemn "homosexuality" when the precedents prohibit at most certain acts. Church statements, reports, and proposals move without reflection from talking about condemned acts to stigmatizing categories of persons designated by one or another scientific terminology. More: Passages on the definition of sexual categories simply yield to contemporary scientists and their preferred terminology. A 1977 statement by the Office of Research and Analysis of the American Lutheran Church refers questions about the prevalence, origin, and pathology of "homosexuality" to "the various scientific disciplines," which are expected "to debate and resolve" them.[22] While it awaits the scientific results, the statement does not hesitate to apply a string of biblical passages first to "homosexual behavior" and then to the "homosexual person."

Amid the confusions, where and how does the notion of "sexual identity" take hold in denominational statements? The question is tricky because the meanings are so confused. For example, in 1970 the General Assembly of the United Presbyterian Church in the United States circulated but did not endorse a congregational study document that

introduces "male and female homosexuality" with a psychological primer:

> In the course of a normal pattern of growth, there are
> many factors which influence the shaping of one's
> [1] *sexual identity. . . .* There is a development process
> . . . the end of which is the establishment of a [2] *com-*
> *fortable identity* with one's given sexuality. . . . In
> some persons' development process, these homosex-
> ual feelings and experiences become fixed as the [3]
> *definition of their sexual identity.*[23]

The first italicized phrase borrows "identity" from Erikson
to name a developing sense of one's gender (as we would
say). It is followed immediately by a reference to God's creation of male and female. The second italicized phrase
means "identity" as congruity. In the third italicized phrase,
it is unclear whether "definition" refers to a biopsychological
process or to a speech act, and the meaning of "sexual identity" is—I cannot guess.

And so on. A reader may conclude that some denominational statements from the 1970s deploy key terms without
taking the trouble to be clear about what they mean—or to
wonder where they come from, since they evidently descend
neither from the Christian scriptures nor from older bodies
of church law and theology. Even so, a reader should notice
the growing reliance on the terminology of sexual identity—
perhaps because it is intrinsically confused.

Reverse Use

The tolerant accommodations in progressive church documents contrast with the fierce disapproval of some evangelical speech from the 1970s. The contrast in influence can
seem just as sharp. Among all of the decade's discussions of

sexual identity, one of the most widely read in the United States must be *The Anita Bryant Story* (1977).

Ghostwritten soon after her victory over a Dade County nondiscrimination ordinance, the mass market book narrates Bryant's awakening to the threat of organized homosexuality. As part of this education, Bryant comes to accept as an authority the antifeminist tract *Sexual Suicide*, from which she quotes and paraphrases extensively. "[The book] describes homosexuality as a 'flight from identity and love,' the 'gay liberation' movement as an 'escape from sexual responsibility [that threatens] millions of young men who have precarious masculine identities.'"[24] Bryant doubles this sociopolitical authority with the medicalized judgment of Charles Socarides. She then makes the terminology her own: "*God has ordained sexual identities* innate in male and female; so homosexuality is a twisting of divine order" (107, emphasis added).

The context makes clear that Bryant means by "sexual identity" a divine ordering as male or female—one or the other without remainder. Bryant does not learn the word "homosexual" to distinguish a desire or attraction from its expression in acts. She heads in the opposite direction: She thinks of the acts through the twisting of identity. When she wants to express her utter disgust at sex between men, she uses the odd locution "the act of homosexuality" (67). She is describing an explicit photograph sent to her anonymously. What it depicts is too terrible for details. She can only tell her readers that it was . . . the *act* of *homosexuality*. She does not want people just to refrain from acts; she wants them to cease being the sort of person capable of doing those acts. (Her original subtitle was *One Woman's Fight against the Sin of Homosexuality*.) The identity is the problem—I mean, the target of unspeakable disgust.

In Bryant and later evangelical writers, the language of a divinely ordained "sexual identity" underwrites claims for cures. The most theoretical claim comes from Elizabeth Moberly, the author of two books published in 1983. The first culls psychoanalytic theories to argue that male homosexuality is caused by a damaging "disidentification" from the father that leads to a "deficit" in relation to males or maleness.[25] Money and Stoller figure as important authorities in *Psychogenesis*. So does Otto Fenichel, a systematizer of psychoanalytic orthodoxy. Moberly's second book applies her account of gender identity to Christian ethics. Her main claim is that homosexuality, like transsexuality, is "a problem of gender identity" and, more specifically, of "an incomplete same-sex identity."[26] Moberly's account of identity in homosexuality is many times more technical than Anita Bryant's, but both have the effect of anchoring Christian teaching about sex in a theory of identities. The theory is transmuted instantaneously into theology. For Bryant, "God has ordained sexual identities." For Moberly, "God did not create homosexuals as homosexuals, but as men and women who are intended to attain psychological maturity in their gender identity"—and who have so far failed to do so (*H*, 30). On both accounts, identity becomes a more fundamental category for Christian theology than it was for radical or progressive writers.

If this reinterpretation of identity can be attributed to differences in progressive and evangelical temperaments, it also shows the opposed rhetoric of affirmation and condemnation. A Christian *affirmation* of homosexuality, inspired by Bailey, may hold that the canonical scriptures have nothing explicit to say about innate homosexuality as a moral topic—or may argue, as Elizabeth Stuart does, that baptism erases all merely social identities.[27] By contrast, a severe Christian *condemnation* of homosexuality must suppose that homosexuality is an adequate theological description for something that merits *damnation*. "Sexual identity" has moved from the clinic to the streets to the soul. We are how we copulate—by divine decree. But that description only reinforces the underlying question: How to explain this rapid adoption, across a range of churchly viewpoints, of such a problematic neologism as "sexual identity"?

Here is a first explanation. For most of modernity, various Christian theologies have negotiated for control over sex with emerging medical and scientific theories. Foucault refers to the famous transfer of power from Christian pastoral practice to modern medicine, not least in psychology or psychiatry. Whether or not you accept Foucault's grand narrative, it is certainly worth noting that theologians since the end of the nineteenth century have simultaneously rejected new sciences of sex and borrowed their conclusions. (We have just seen this in Moberly.) The rapid appropriation of "sexual identity" may be another round in an ongoing game of catch-up. The longer the game goes on, the more important it becomes to ask which insights of its own Christianity brings to discussions of human sexuality.

A second explanation for the rapid adoption of sexual identities by churches would look to the particular relations between progressive or liberal forms of Christianity and various liberation movements in the 1960s. The complex interconnections of African American "civil rights," feminism, and "gay liberation" are now well studied. So, too, are efforts by some Christians and their churches to join or support the movements. It is not a surprise, then, that progressive Christian theologians adopt the terminology of their allies. Of course, this leaves unexplained the adoption of "sexual identity" and similar terms by (so-called) conservative Christian groups. It also raises questions, as above, about what Christianity offers in return to movements for sexual "liberation."

The third explanation may seem remote, but I find it the most interesting. Some years ago, at the conclusion of a book on the origins and early history of the theological category of sodomy, I proposed: "Because Latin theologians thought in terms of Sodomites, we have found it so easy to think of ourselves as *being* homosexuals, as having a lesbian or gay *identity*." What I meant was that "the idea of an identity built around the genital configuration of one's sexual partners is, in our traditions, the product of Christian theology."[28] If I were writing those sentences today, I would not use "identity"—at least, not without cautions. My point may still stand. Christian theologians have often been experts in polemic, and they learned to personify sins or heresies as memorable targets for condemnation. Peter Damian, whom I credit with putting the term "sodomy" into wide circulation, invented the theological abstraction by imagining, ever more gruesomely, the figure of the Sodomite. Sex/gender identities are also personifications—clinical rather than scriptural, but still polemical. Having trafficked so long in moralizing figures, Christian writers were well prepared to take up a new one—even from their modern rivals.

Whatever the causes or motives behind the spread of sexual identities through Christian thinking, I regard it as unfortunate. Identity-language for sex/gender contains too many troublesome contradictions and implications. It carries bad habits of literal speech. Most problematically for theology, it caps or limits human aspirations. If a sexual identity is at once the core of your being and what joins you to social expectations or political movements, how can it enable you to transcend whichever powers run the social and political?

PART II
Recalling Spirits

4

Ancestral Prophecies, Future Myths

For as long as there has been a "movement" in defense of civil rights for homoerotic love, there have been quarrels over what kind of history should be told about it. That might seem too obvious to be worth saying. *Of course* defenders of sexual criminalization view such movements as indecent campaigns for perversion or lewdness, hardly worth the attention of serious political historians. *Of course* advocates of decriminalization narrate their efforts as a necessary extension of human rights. But I am thinking of the quarrels within queer communities about their own narratives of progress or regress. Are these histories only social and political? Are they also artistic, literary, ethical—perhaps spiritual?

The archives make one thing clear: Much influential writing on behalf of queer flourishing from 1970 forward has been frankly mythological. It understood the progress of queer lives to depend upon recovering ancestral memories and anticipating more-than-secular futures. If it was a political movement, its politics embraced magic and called forth poetic prophecy.

I pull from the shelves four examples, published over the years when identity language was staking its claims both in queer politics and in Christian groups: Mary Daly's *Beyond God the Father*, Audre Lorde's *Zami*, Judy Grahn's *Another Mother Tongue*, and Gloria Anzaldúa's *Borderlands/La Frontera*. I consider them so many prologues to an unusually erotic spirituality.

If I choose four texts by women, I do not mean to induct them into a false universality that is tacitly male (or white). There are no universal languages for sex/gender, only languages that pretend to be. There is also no eternal canon. Lifting up just these four books, I testify to their power as teachers of language for me. I reiterate the caution against universality for the word "spirituality." The word has many meanings in the four texts listed. Sometimes the authors try to sort these. At other times, they trust that the undefined word can still lead a reader to important recognitions or embodied experiences. The word's uses matter much more than dictionary-style definitions. They suggest that spirituality itself is more concerned with active transformations than propositional conclusions. Indeed, the language of spirit is more persuasion or direction than theses and information.

In an essay on silence first published in 1967, Susan Sontag inserts this parenthesis: "Spirituality = plans, terminologies, ideas of deportment aimed at resolving the painful structural contradictions inherent in the human situation, at the completion of human consciousness, at transcendence."[1] Fifteen years later, Foucault claims the word at the start of a public lecture series: Spirituality will name "the ensemble of those searches, practices, and experiences that may include purifications, ascetical practices, renunciations, redirections of gaze, modifications of existence, etc., [and] which constitute, not for knowledge but for the subject, for the very being of the subject, the price to be paid for access to the truth."[2]

Each of these provocative formulations sets a sort of goal: for Sontag, "completion" or "transcendence"; for Foucault, "access to the truth." The goal is less distinctive than the ways to it. For Sontag, these include "terminologies" and "ideas of deportment"—or how you talk and how you act, move, inhabit your body. For Foucault, the means are "searches, practices, and experiences" that alter "the very being of the subject." He explains, in the lines following, that influential accounts describe the alteration as movement and bodily training or art. Once altered, the seeker is able to encounter truth as illumination, a gift of tranquility, a blessedness. For Foucault, as for Sontag, spirituality's transformation begins by shifting both the forms and purposes of language. It is like turning from the prose of proof to the poetry of guidance.

Daly: Myths for an Exodus (1973/1985)

In severe review, Mary Daly would repudiate some of the basic tenets of her *Beyond God the Father*. I acknowledge that repudiation and will return to it. But I start with the book as it first appeared in 1973, because that version shows more clearly Daly's original motives for remaking language.

Daly begins by dismissing previous Christian thought: "The entire conceptual systems of theology and ethics, developed under the conditions of patriarchy, have been the products of males and tend to serve the interests of sexist society."[3] This rejection leads to a positive proposal for writing anew at the border of philosophy and theology. Instead of trying to fix inherited systems or their concepts, Daly continues,

> it seems to me far more important to listen to women's experiences to discover the spiritual dynamics of this revolution and to speak these dynamics in our

own lives and words. . . . This does not mean that an
entirely new language of God, materially speaking,
will emerge, *ex nihilo*, but rather that a new meaning
context is coming into being as we re-create our lives
in a new experiential context.

(37)

The parallel between "new meaning context" and "new
experiential context" recalls the common commitment to
make a language out of women's experience ("in our own
lives and words"). The reverse is also true: "The spiritual
dynamics of this revolution" will enable new forms of life
not yet visible or habitable. A woman trying to voice her
experience now must expect that her life will be changed by
spiritual forces that transform women's communities even as
she speaks. Daly connects the effort "to break out of the iron
mask of language forms that are strangling us" with the call
for an exodus from male-dominated institutions. "The adequate exodus requires communication, community, and
creation" (167, 158). I take the alliterative trio to mean that
revolutionary exodus calls women to communicate with one
another in communities that create new forms of language
and life.

The call to remake language in altered communities is
the persistent exhortation of *Beyond God the Father*. A reader
can see something more of how Daly carried it out in the
introduction that she added twelve years later—the "Original Reintroduction." *Original*, because Daly underscores
her claims on pre-patriarchal wisdom, which flourished
before the beginnings of Civilization. *Reintroduction*,
because Daly writes from an ongoing exodus, during the
journey of her own reeducation. She translates herself
into the new language as she shapes it. So, Daly corrects
her earlier vocabulary—say, with regard to "androgyny" or

"homosexuality." She views those words in retrospect as transitional or self-liquidating, but she wants to correct more than single words. She will find or compose language strong enough to deploy divine powers.

How? One obvious feature of Daly's new language is etymological punning. She writes words otherwise—capitalizing or rehyphenating them. She also redefines certain words (Background), recoins them (Be-Friending), or dislocates them by reversing their ordinary meanings. Doing all of that, she reveals the haunting presence of another language alongside patriarchal edicts. For Daly, language is the path of exodus, a strip of dry land opened between the waters of the blood-colored patriarchal sea—a way into the other Time and Space of women's esoteric traditions.

A reader should note two other features of Daly's writing. One is the reiterated emphasis on practice or experience—and, indeed, on modes of experience beyond ordinary perception or reasoning. With some adjustment of the word, *Beyond God the Father* is best read as a "mystical" text. Daly's writing of visionary exodus is *not* like the texts of the medieval Christian women usually called "mystical" (in part to segregate them from the canon of mainstream theology). Hildegard of Bingen, Hadewijch, Mechthild, and Margaret Porete push prose and poetry to their limits when registering the shocks of divine encounter. Daly is not that kind of writer. She is closer to an author like Teresa of Avila, who writes plainly, even domestically, to unleash a prolific imagination, vivid yet always shifting. But even that comparison is inexact. Daly is a *Scholastic* mystic: She remains fascinated by the multiple meanings of words, the comparison and cataloguing of competing vocabularies, and the projection of larger pedagogical structures. A lexicon of key words that dissects meanings and proposes radical corrections is an eminently Scholastic genre that goes back to Aristotle.

Daly also proposes new language for liturgy or ritual. I call it "magical" in hopes that you can hear the word neutrally, neither pejoratively nor dismissively. One liturgical example is the formula that concludes Daly's "Original Reintroduction": "The Journey can and does continue because the Verb continues—from whom, in whom and with whom all true movements move" (xxix). Here Daly rewrites the conclusion of a Christian Eucharistic prayer: "through the same Jesus Christ our Lord; by whom, and with whom, and in whom, in the unity of the Holy Ghost all honor and glory be unto thee, O Father Almighty." A very patriarchal Trinity becomes, in Daly's re-vision, the Verb moving women to speak otherwise. More: A Eucharistic formula is not just any prayer. It is a prayer that professes to transform human lives by changing a corner of the world— on some traditional theologies, by making this bread and wine into the body and blood of a divine savior. It links a present moment to the singular event of the savior's last evening of teaching. Rewriting the Eucharistic doxology, Daly suggests that her language has the power of a sacramental formula. She invites expelled powers back into history.

Lorde: Experiments in Biomythography (1982)

Audre Lorde's *Zami* has a subtitle, *A New Spelling of My Name*.[4] The book explains: "Zami. A Carriacou name for women who work together as friends and lovers" (255). What kind of name is it—proper (as Lorde adopts it), common, allegorical? And why does she relate it to her other names as an alternate spelling rather than a renaming? The cover of another edition inserts a phrase before the author's name: *A Biomythography*.[5] The book is a myth about the life of (a?) Zami. The myth is richly layered, complicated in telling and reading. Here, as so often, I must choose passages—only two, in fact. I pick them out almost as if they were scriptural verses that speak directly to urgent practical questions. Then I meditate on them—gloss them, medieval theologians would say—by attaching other passages from Lorde. Is this a responsible interpretation of the whole book? Of course not. I hope for another sort of learning.

The first passage falls more than two-thirds of the way into the book. It reads,

> In those days, whenever two or more lesbians got together, the most frequent topic of conversation was "Do you think she's gay?" . . . Always before, the few lesbians I had known were women whom I had met within other existing contexts of life. We shared some part of a world common to us both—school or work or poetry or some other interest beyond our sexual identity.
>
> (196)

This seems to be the book's only mention of "sexual identity." That is interesting in itself—as an indicator for usage in Lorde and the communities around her. More interesting, for me, is an extraordinary passage thirty pages later. It is printed entirely in italics:

> *Being women together was not enough. We were different. Being gay-girls together was not enough. We were different. Being Black together was not enough. We were different. Being Black women together was not enough. We were different. Being Black dykes together was not enough. We were different.*
>
> (226)

A few lines later, she adds, without italics: "It was a while before we came to realize that our place was the very house of difference rather [than] the security of any one particular difference." The very house of difference: the latent architecture of *Zami*. The book begins and ends with dreams of sex/gender fusion, raced embodiments, memories of misrecognition, and the will to learn. But it also ties *Zami* or being (a) Zami to Lorde's other texts, especially the unforgettable essay "The Uses of the Erotic."

"Uses" was originally delivered, in the late summer of 1978, to the fourth Berkshire Conference on the History of Women at Mt. Holyoke College. When she rose to speak, Lorde was well-known as a poet. Some months before the lecture, she had published *The Black Unicorn* (January 1978). That book also attempts a mythology for Lorde's life and some lives near it. You can feel the urgency of this language-effort in the last lines of the poem, "A Litany for Survival": "So it is better to speak/remembering/we were never meant to survive." The movement of the poem to the last line accomplishes a survival by declaring it. The poem's title suggests another accomplishment: "A *Litany* for Survival." A litany is a repetitive liturgical poem that typically unrolls in call and response. Lorde's poem is a prayer in aid of praying—as so many prayers are. It is a litany that must answer itself.

"The Uses of the Erotic" extends the litany into a teaching about flourishing. When your life must be preoccupied with survival, when every poem you write must be part of that embodied litany, what is the use of the erotic? Perhaps you should regard sexual love as a distraction, a narcotic, or a tragedy—for yourself, your lovers, the children that might be born. What is the use? Wittgenstein would translate: What meaning does your use give to "erotic"? Lorde enumerates three uses: "providing the power which comes from sharing deeply any pursuit with another person," "the open and fearless underlining of my capacity for joy," and a joyful "demand from all of my life that it be lived within the knowledge that such satisfaction is possible, and does not have to be called marriage, nor god, nor an afterlife."[6] The first use is Lorde's reply to older efforts to confine the erotic to reproductive unions, preferably those blessed by the state, the church, or the state-church. There is indeed union, Lorde says. It is the power that comes from sharing—not just sexual sharing but any deep communion. Sharing connects to joy. Erotic joy is in turn an ethical imperative—a "demand"—for the rest of life. The rest of life should be animated and measured by the ethical knowing that comes from erotic experience. Erotic ethics is strong politics. More: It is a spirituality that flourishes apart from creeds about divinities or guarantees of immortality.

Touching the power of the erotic requires discernment—and, in a highly sexualized market society, the discipline of setting aside the pornographic simulacra of the erotic, "plasticized" sensations. I connect the contrast erotic/pornographic with Lorde's allusions to mythic accounts of Eros as a divinity. She recalls that Eros is "born of Chaos . . . personifying creative power and harmony." Talk of gods and cosmogonies issues in a correction: "It has become fashionable to separate the spiritual (psychic and emotional) from the political, to see them as contradictory or antithetical. . . . In the same way, we have attempted to separate the spiritual and the erotic, thereby reducing the spiritual to a world of flattened affect, a world of the ascetic who aspires to feel nothing" (SO, 55–56). The erotic is not the pornographic, but it must be both political and spiritual.

After many years of teaching this essay, I am convinced that it uses "spiritual" as an enigmatic placeholder for power sensed only in deep emotion. "The erotic cannot be felt secondhand" (SO, 59). Lorde has experienced it firsthand with a particular body—in a room of her own within the house of difference. Her eloquent advocacy for certain groups, her participation in political actions—both grow from a richer sharing of bodily experiences, some (most?) on a spiritual plane. Silenced for so long, in so many ways, Lorde's erotic life has barely begun to speak itself. The first thing it says is: We need a different language—with other assumptions about the unities implied by naming.

I am brought back to the second passage in *Zami*. One of Lorde's best-known pieces of political advice is this: "Unity does not require that we be identical to each other."[7] She spoke that line to a roomful of other Black women when she wanted to persuade them that she lived her life simultaneously as Black, feminist, lesbian—and, to add other labels she sometimes used, as mother, poet, and warrior. Just as she articulated herself through these different roles or identities, she could work with them in shared political commitments. She could also write them all with a "power behind my voice" (Z, 3).

What is the *sound* of the spiritual/erotic? Lorde's prose texts are notable for their simplicity. They grip language in ways one expects from a poet but otherwise rely on direct exhortation. How can that be—since Lorde has called so eloquently for the making of new language, for claiming suppressed experience through language? Do her lectures or essays mean to lure readers back into poetry as the more spiritual language? Lorde might answer that such questions assume false divisions: between poetry and prose, between telling and teaching, between *bios* and *mythos*. The power behind the voice is not a particular skill with word patterns. It is the life of a body grounded in erotic spirit. The body tells the myth by living it and then recalling it in song—say, the prose-poem of *Zami*.

Grahn: The Poetry of Before (1984)

Judy Grahn's *Another Mother Tongue* begins by quoting "Two Loves" by Alfred Douglas. That poem, recall, ends with the line that echoes through so many queer texts (including this one): "I am the Love that dare not speak its name." Grahn's searing poem "A Woman Is Talking to Death" begins with the line "Testimony in trials that never got heard." The space between the two poems is the painful hope of queer naming. The love that dare not speak its name/the love that speaks without ever being heard. The love that has no audible name—which is no single name at all.

Judy Grahn has done many things, written much, joined or founded several creative communities. Let me take a single example to stand for many: a poetry workshop that began in 1967 at San Francisco's Society for Individual Rights, a homophile organization. The workshop was both a space for making new languages and a site from which to broadcast them. With Robert Duncan as its advisor, the group drew writers who would go on to produce influential work. It was the cradle for *Man-Root*, a poetry journal, which published in its first eight issues work by Kathy Acker, James Broughton, Marilyn Hacker, Denise Levertov, and Paul Mariah (its chief editor), along with Genet in fresh translation. Grahn contributed three poems to the very first issue of *Man-Root*. One describes (remembers, imagines) climbing to the "Sandia Man Cave." It is a tricky hike even for regular walkers: half a mile up the side of Las Huertas canyon on the east slope of the Sandias. At the end, you are on ledges and metal stairs. Then you reach the cave that was a human house ten thousand years ago. Grahn writes: "my ancestors/i could crawl up the cliff face/to meet you/but my toes are misshapen/we are all born with shoes on."[8] Language for sexed human bodies is a closetful of ill-fitting shoes.

In *Another Mother Tongue*, Grahn climbs to other ancestors—the generations of queer folk, especially women, who made language in hollowed-out spaces where sounds were already discounted as gibberish (to paraphrase Foucault's original preface to *History of Madness*). The neglected trail that Grahn follows in the book is marked by puzzling words that still circulate in queer vernaculars. Speaking of her first lover, Vonne (the book's muse), Grahn writes: "She taught me the words of Gay life; she could not tell me what they meant."[9] Certain words are like tokens passed from hand to hand, incised with runes that no one alive can read. Grahn imagines a spoken transmission, an "oral history we heard in a line passed on from our first lover's first lover's first lover" (3).

Grahn believes—as Harry Hay did—in persisting queer cultures. She locates "Gayness" in cultural transmission rather than in desires for specific sexual acts. "We have a history, or more appropriately several histories, that give our way of life meaning beyond its simple mechanics." Grahn draws the consequences for sexual politics: "Being a Lesbian is more than a 'political choice' made by consciously feminist women of the seventies." The urgent task is to reassemble the remains of drowned or burned or muzzled language. Forgotten Gay wisdom cannot be reduced to politics, sociology, psychology: "If Gayness has a culture of its own, it exists in the midst of but is not caused by any of those [social] conditions" (17–19). Identity cards will *not* be issued. Indeed, Grahn does not rely on the notion "sexual identity." If she speaks of identification with one thing or another, she does not speak of identities.

The main work of *Another Mother Tongue* is archeological repair. Convinced of the living unity of gay culture, Grahn moves from place to place, time to time. Much of her history is "wrong" by academic standards, and her leaps from text to text would make a philologist cringe. The objection is beside her point. She uses modernist collage to revivify "the Old Religion." That Religion is everywhere in Grahn's book. At the beginning, right after quoting Douglas, she hears in her lover's whispers "the forbidden litany of who we were or might be" (3). Litany, again. The most familiar litany in Western churches is the "Litany of the Saints," which calls on holy women and men from early Christian centuries for protection from a host of human evils. *Another Mother Tongue* is yet another queer litany. It is liturgy—or incantation, spell, initiation. "Our belonging to a secret, different world and way of life" means standing "at the gate between the land of material flesh in one world and the land of the spirit or soul in another" (14, 6). A more than visible house of difference.

Grahn's book ends in New York with a concert for the queer dead. Some of her work is sung alongside the poetry of five other "Gay" authors, including Walt Whitman. The contralto begins to sing "Funeral Plainsong," as Grahn calls her poem in shorthand.[10] She feels the presence of her first lover, her tutor in queer speech: "You were there, Von, for I felt you . . . and something grand was happening, something ceremonial . . . with something like the Gay sound of a piccolo following you down your spirit trail like a golden butterfly, singing rainbow songs . . . (i will be your mouth now, to do your singing)" (*AMT*, 284). Grahn is quoting her own poetry. She "quotes" by speaking again words that she receives as Lesbian inheritance.

"Funeral Plainsong" is part of *She Who*, published as a chapbook with illustrations and photographs of women who are acknowledged, memorialized, transfigured. The poem's endnote says: "for ritual use only." The instruction could apply to the whole of *She Who*. In retrospect, Grahn says of her "Funeral Song": "In such ways we begin to reclaim the events of our own lives, as well as making our poetry what it should be and once was: specific, scientific, valuable, of real use" (*WCW*, 76).

For the collection of Grahn's poetry written from 1964 to 1977, Adrienne Rich writes an introduction. She describes Grahn reading "Funeral Song" to a New York gathering on a winter night in 1974. She says, "As long as our language is inadequate, our vision remains formless, our thinking and feeling are still running in the old cycles, our process may be 'revolutionary' but not transformative" (WCW, 7). Among the words of the old cycles: "homosexual" (14). More adequate language is discovered or invented (two related verbs) by poetry. "Poetry is, among other things, a criticism of language. . . . Poetry is above all a concentration of the *power* of language." Beginning and ending, Rich's introduction repeats, "The necessity of poetry has to be stated over and over, but only to those . . . who still believe the language is 'only words'" (8, 7, 21).

Before telling how "Funeral Song" was sung, Grahn mentions Gay translations of lost religious knowledge. She foresees the Lesbian future as cultivation of supraculture, metaculture, transculture. "What we perhaps have at the core is an uncanny ability to identify with what we are not, to die as one form and return as another. . . . All the more so since we cannot say our names" (AMT, 274). The capacity for identification, for becoming other, is not an identity. In Grahn's mythology, the magical ability to take on lost languages is joined to the inability to speak one's own name. You can channel oracles or be "ridden" by old divinities because you do not have a single, speakable name. "I am approaching the ceremonial state as a dike and can consider myself on the way to becoming something of a modern ceremonial Lesbian in spite of our fractured modern society" (281). A ceremonial Lesbian is a Lesbian who writes old words and new by ritual mimicry and making. It is a spiritual vocation if ever there was one.

Anzaldúa: Many-Tongued Border Gods (1987)

Gloria Evangelina Anzaldúa published *Borderlands/La Frontera* with the women's press Spinsters/Aunt Lute. An earlier anthology, *This Bridge Called My Back*, coedited by Cherríe Moraga and Anzaldúa, had been produced in 1981 by Persephone Press, which also brought out Lorde's *Zami*. The network of small women's presses, with their calendars of authors' events, both encouraged and shared experiments in language.

Borderlands/La Frontera zigzags—as you should expect from its title. There is a detailed outline in the table of contents, but the arc of narrative or argument (they intertwine) is hard to plot. The first part of the book intercuts an autobiography with an academic monograph—flouting the rules of both genres. The book's second part collects poems under six headings. The headings narrate a life pattern, but the poems under them are more loosely arranged. I won't try to solve the book's structure as if it were a puzzle. Instead, I follow a few paths through it. Label them Land, Language, Testimony, and Myth. They are so many approaches to conversations with queer gods.

LAND. *Borderlands* is preoccupied with geographies—with land and the people who give their years to it. Anzaldúa was born in far south Texas, near McAllen. Along that reach, if you are close to the river or the Gulf of Mexico, you discover palms and extravagant animals: birds with red faces, rose throats, sulfur-yellow bellies, bodies of iridescent green-yellow and heads almost indigo. Away from the water, you move through cactus, mesquite, *guajillo* (catclaw), *palo blanco* (sugarberry), lizards, tarantulas, armadillos, javelinas, coyotes, rattlesnakes—under a sky blanched by sun.

As Anzaldúa makes plain, the Rio Grande (or Río Bravo) is an utterly unconvincing national boundary. The river marks no old differences of culture, language, ethnicity, or religion. It is just where a flag was planted at the end of a series of land grabs during the nineteenth century. Long-time residents along the Rio became, overnight, subjects of the United States—bound to another government, its northern language, and its bookish Protestantism. In Anzaldúa, *la frontera* is an unhealed cut through words.

LANGUAGE. Which words can describe that cut? Anzaldúa uses many languages—official Spanish and English, of course, but also their dialects, slangs, improvisations, collisions. There are words from Nahuatl, spoken now mostly in central Mexico, but in its older form the language of the Aztec gods. The spiritual wound opened by the border reveals the "historical/mythological" space of Aztlán: the fabled homeland, the Aztec Eden.[11] It is, for Anzaldúa, also the queer space of the *Atravesados*, "those who cross over, pass over, or go through confines of the 'normal.'" The land's cut doubles the people born onto it. "But I, like other queer people, am two in one body, both male and female" (*B/F*, 25, 41). Or, in the local slang, *mita' y mita'*, half and half.

TESTIMONY. Anzaldúa's book harvests testimonies. It rages against crimes, both personal and social. It laments the scars of poverty, the daily violence, the deaths. But the book also bears spiritual witness. Faced with corrupt police and a finely attired border patrol, Anzaldúa discovers within herself the Shadow-Beast, a figure at once of resistance and lust (38, 42). The wailing of local women is doubled by La Llorona, the weeping mother of Mexican folklore. (I learned about her as a boy growing up, far south of the Río, in the central Mexican highlands.) You can hear La Llorona in strong winds, hunting for her lost children—or coming to avenge them. The borderland's spirits need long memories. Tenacious remembering is one way to resist the self-promotion of empires.

Anzaldúa gives more personal testimony. As a child, she was bitten by a rattlesnake while working the fields. Because she survived, she counted the bite as a claim on her by Snake Woman, serpent-goddess—known also as Coatlicue, Coyolxauhqui, Tonantsi, Tlazolteatl, Cihuacoatl. With the bite, she is inducted as servant and messenger by a family of female divinities, "the old spirit entities" (53).

Sometimes Anzaldúa describes the claim psychologically, as a "mental picture and symbol of the instinctual in its collective impersonal, pre-human." In the next moment, she accepts the claim to enter an alternate reality: "We're supposed [under the US empire] to ignore, forget, kill those fleeting images of the soul's presence and of the spirit's presence. . . . We're supposed to forget that every cell in our bodies, every bone and bird and worm has spirit in it." The snake's bite inaugurates a lifetime of messages, omens, visions. It grants *la facultad*, "the capacity to see in surface phenomena the meaning of deeper realities. . . . Those who are pounced on the most have it the strongest—the females, the homosexuals of all races, the darkskinned, the outcast, the persecuted, the marginalized, the foreign" (57–58, 60). For Anzaldúa, in this passage, "the homosexuals of all races" possess more frequently and intensely than some others a spiritual gift. (I would add: Homosexuality is not, of course, the same sort of thing across "all races"—but neither is race.) For the groups that she mentions, there is no opposition between the call of the goddesses and the political work to be done. A *facultad* enables politics.

MYTH. Theology as mythology insinuates itself into Anzaldúa's most political analyses. The conflict of cultures brings about "a new hybrid race" that "never existed before" (27). Anzaldúa's use of *la raza* goes back to José Vasconcelos.[12] I make better sense of *Borderlands* if I detach the notion of a cosmic race from Vasconcelos to connect it with promises made by spirit-women, Aztec goddesses, figures of folklore,

adaptations of the Virgin Mary. Under their patronage, Anzaldúa combines geography, languages, and suffered history
into a new mythology. If Anzaldúa is rightly claimed as an
inspiration for political activism, she is even more—in this
book at least—another lesbian mythographer. Her sexuality
(to intrude an alien word) made her all the more susceptible
to ongoing revelation. Hear that: "Sexuality" or "sexual orientation" is a gift for prophecy. Anzaldúa's desire for other
women is also, she keeps claiming, a queer calling—a vocation in the old Catholic sense.

Borderlands does not end with a chapter on *mestiza* consciousness. It ends with a hundred pages of poetry—some in
English, some in English and Spanish, some only in Spanish. The fifth sheaf of poems, *"Animas"* (Souls), tells of res-
urrections, possessions, spiritual apprenticeships, hungry
ghosts, cactus women, and sex with goddesses. A deliberate
retrieval of anachronistic myths? A flight into mystification?
Or is the second half of Anzaldúa's book actually the more
important—the place in which queer politics finds its deeper
grounding in a poetics?

Varieties of Queer Spirituality

How many times "spirituality" has occurred in connection
with queer efforts at naming and mythmaking, with how
many senses! No single definition could cover all or even
most of the word's uses. No single definition could get at the
power(s) behind it. Still, I remain curious about the repeated
choice of "spirituality" by such different authors to protect
possibilities of queer transformation. Their shared vocabulary is not merely religious residue, masked childhood yearn-
ing, or compensatory resistance. The turns to "spirituality"
register instead something of the giddy and frightening

effort to write what happens when a queer self is released into the play of strange powers.

Here is a first attempt to sort the meanings—which begs to be corrected. "Spirituality" performs clusters of functions. One cluster highlights *ritual* in the creation of sexual characters as alternatives to medico-legal identities. (Take "ritual" most broadly: It may include cooking or hammering together; it certainly includes dancing, singing, and sex.) The languages, practices, and communities we classify as religions cultivate practices we count as rituals to sustain characters that direct sexual desire or activity. Because religions police bodily boundaries, they become expert in fashioning characters for narrating significance in bodies. That expertise can be deployed for many purposes, including overturning the prevailing medical, social, or political categories.

A second cluster of functions for "spirituality" *juxtaposes* beliefs and practices from historical religions, real or fantasized. The word gives license to inhabit multiple ritual systems. There is a lesson here about the complexity of ritual characters in modern times, another about the alleged opposition of secular and sacred. Queer folk joke about their piety toward sex clubs or camps, dance floors, Pride parades, and music festivals. Of course, they are not joking.

A third cluster of functions is the most interesting to me. "Spirituality" is used to *protect* some part of erotic experience from medico-scientific and legal-political terminologies. It tries to prevent sex from being seized by the dominant experts and their police—the inquisitors of scientific medicine or political platforms, the vice squad or the censors of some Movement. To live present or past decades in the United States as an "openly" queer person is to become a hypervisible body with a hypersexuality or hypergender. A claim of spirituality can provide the shelter of mystery. Still, it is striking that bodily hopes are entrusted to spirit. Spirit points toward the "free territory" in which bodies can express what they have hidden—right on the skin.[13]

Queer spiritualities are not linked by a single concept, definition, or doctrine. They resemble one another in the resistance or improvisation they authorize. The shared, stubborn faith is that communities of sexual practice might open spaces for encountering invisible powers. Orgasm becomes epiphany. If you judge that a tawdry joke, I remind you that one of the first gay sex manuals, *Men Loving Men*, ends with a section entitled "Mystical Aspects of Gay Love." A single sample from it: "What's the nature of this [male-male] love, and why does it seem so wonderful? I think it's because it unlocks the secret reality, the secret self inside each of us, and provides a doorway to revelations."[14] Not *the* doorway, but one of many, opening from branching halls in hundreds of houses. Houses of difference here, too.

Archives of queer language dream of names in harmony with fine arts of bodily practice, with new poetries, and with the pursuit of the uncontainable evoked by human sex. The bodily practice may sometimes look scandalous—but then transforming ritual, taken seriously, often gives scandal. The poetry may be dismissed as merely literary—but then we often turn to "literature" for ethical instruction. The haunting memory of the uncontainable points to horizons of aspiration, not least in the face of death.

5
Other Regimens of Bodies and Pleasures

In gossip, in interviews, in memes, specific bodily disciplines—from women's softball to *haute coiffure*—are fused with queerness. Those clichés are jokingly familiar. Other body arts, less mundane, less polite, continue to remake queer languages. They offer scripts for scenes that turn present bodies toward future characters. Or they contribute to the pages of slowly materializing dictionaries.[1] If this book has all along struggled with fugitive gaps between words and bodies, it does so especially when it attends to bodily disciplines. Here too, I will juxtapose small pieces of text that register quite different uses of bodies. The uses are neither easy nor obvious. Before you could interpret any of them confidently, your body would have to learn a larger discipline. My tentative hope remains that textual collage will show why some queer people stylize their bodies to speak otherwise of other lives.

Leather Liturgies

Urban Aboriginals by Geoff Mains (1984) is a landmark "celebration" of leather communities. I will return to its easily offensive title, but I start further back. Since the book presents itself as the record of a journey, at once travelogue and pocket guide, I approach it through another sort of itinerary: Mains's journals. Authorial biography is not the spell to unlock every text, but it gains importance here through the claim that leather requires bodily training into commitment. That claim should remind readers that Mains's language does not work quite like a story about going to buy five red apples—unless "apples" is a euphemism.

The journals: While an undergraduate at the University of Toronto, Mains rejects his childhood Christianity in favor of a "'spiritualism' in life & beauty."[2] A year later, he records affecting visits to Christian sites in England. They culminate in crisis and recommitment at Yorkminster, an immense Gothic cathedral that glows golden in filtered sunlight. Two years after that, Mains goes to clubs in Toronto and decides finally to "come out." Five years further on—in 1977—he is exploring "leathersex" (his term) and Carlos Castañeda— who becomes, in the book, a demanding model of shamanic initiation. Mains travels regularly to San Francisco, where he begins to frequent the Catacombs, a sex club then located in SoMa.[3] A typical journal entry glides from a group scene at the club to the reminder that he needs "a mystical view of life" and a rediscovery of "magic" (*GMJ*, 12/27/77). It is not surprising to find, some pages later, a poem written to a partner from the Catacombs: "I took your hand in worship / The fingers rimmed with holy fire; / I screamed with relief and joy / To have climbed another cross / And saved another soul" (7/10/78). He takes the hand through his anus.

In a retrospective note covering the decade of the 1970s, T. S. Eliot's "Little Gidding" joins Castañeda to supply language for "self-control, self-respect, and love [of] God. I first found it in the environment, in the dim organ music of York Cathedral in 1970, but later in Christmas, in MCC [Metropolitan Community Church SF], and dear Harvey [Milk]'s death" (*GMJ*, 12/31/79). Mains's papers preserve outlines for an unfinished autobiography in the form of a pilgrimage over a favorite hiking trail. One of the autobiography's planned lessons: "The holy spiritual strength of rock, forest's water."[4] That sort of language appears frequently in the journals. It also runs through the book.

Urban Aboriginals: Both words of the title put off contemporary readers. For Mains, "urban" is not racist code. It means city dweller, and it creates tension with "aboriginal." The title is meant to sound like a contradiction in terms. But what about "aboriginal"? Mains was Canadian and so most likely heard that word as a name for the original inhabitants of Australia and Tasmania. He pairs it with the notion of a journey—perhaps a walkabout. "This book is a journey into the aboriginal soul. . . . It is a journey marked by fetish and mana, shaman, ritual and trance."[5] If the word "aboriginal" threatens to stall your reading, remember that the word is also a quotation: One of his interview subjects uses it to characterize leather practices.[6] Wherever Mains learned the word, he does not give it any pejorative sense. On the contrary, he employs it to praise cultures that are better balanced than ours. So, too, with "tribal": For Mains, that word describes a type of social organization but, even more, practices that are spiritual or magical. However you want to apportion blame, it is fair to say that Mains joins many other White, gay writers in seeking traditional patterns for his own initiation into bodily wisdom.

That puts me in an awkward situation. I never "played" at the Catacombs in any of its locations. Whatever I know of it, I have learned from reading accounts or talking with participants still alive as I wrote. More: I do not count myself a leather man. Does this convict me of indulging ignorant nostalgia for others' pasts without the warrant of initiation? Or does our capacity for learning others' languages complicate dichotomies between insiders and outsiders—as it complicates assessments of appropriation? Who owns a language—in which version, for how long? I have no simple answers to those questions. I can only report that my aim is never to ingest experiences so that I can then claim them as my own. I hope rather to learn the *language* of *Urban Aboriginals* well enough to retell it respectfully.

Mains prefers words like "urban" or "tribal," "spiritual" or "magical," over "Christianity" and even "religion." He acknowledges that some leathermen regard their sexual practices as a new religion. He paraphrases group discussions that show how many more practitioners come from traditional religious backgrounds—as he himself does. Describing leather rituals, sites, and communities, Mains recalls dozens of Christian terms. Among the "faithful," there are priests at their altars before (leather) congregations, novices and disciples in vowed orders. The round of bodily disciplines traces something like the stations of the cross, the itinerary of Jesus's suffering on the way to death. Once in leather paradise, a seeker may intone biblical verses or speak with God. These uses of Christian terms are not metaphorical. They risk blasphemy because Mains means what he says. Even some of his stranger images, like the comparison of crucifixion to giving birth, are theologically traditional. One of the boldest Christian allusions may be concealed in Mains's subtitle: "a celebration of leathersexuality." To celebrate the Eucharist is to transform bread and wine into

Christ's body and blood. For Mains, leathersex is a liturgy with sacraments that change bodily substance.

Not all languages in *Urban Aboriginals* are spiritual. The book borrows models from four discourses: sociological or anthropological ethnography, biomedical explanation, ethical justification, and spiritual exhortation. For ethnography or social description, Mains cites a handful of prominent authors: Benedict and Van Gennep, Goffman and Garfinkel. His biomedical explanations draw from his scientific training and then recent research on endorphins or other natural opioids. Mains's ethical defense claims that leathersex changes people for the better by discharging psychic energies rather than repressing them or diverting them into destructive forms.

Sorting terms in *Urban Aboriginals*, I notice that one phrase does *not* appear: "sexual identity." Mains does write of self-identification in people and groups. Leather tribalism or its practices can supply a shared identity, he says, by affirming a common purpose. But he also reports that the bonds of identities break in ecstasy or trance. Mains quotes an unnamed respondent: "'Whatever I reach, it is magnificent in that space. You are calm like never before above and beyond any identity, timeless'" (*UA*, 97). This awe-filled testimony is a bodily argument against using "sexual identity" without qualifications, including the limits of ordinary space and time.

After many readings of *Urban Aboriginals*, I cannot quite parse its account of bodies and spirits. Sometimes the book elaborates a physiological explanation of the uses of pain— or hallucinogens—to alter consciousness. At other times, it recounts shamanic travel or includes the "occult" alongside shamanism and "oriental religion." Euphoria and ecstasy are real enough for Mains as mental phenomena tied to physical processes, but they are also spiritual realms into which extreme practice hurls the soul. Given all the pages devoted to summarizing science, it can be tempting to label the spiritual, shamanic, or magical idioms as metaphors. But Mains has already complicated "metaphor" by describing it as something that people put on during sex scenes to become other.

I can illustrate the blurring lines with a central preoccupation. *Urban Aboriginals* describes in detail at least three kinds of *space*: the "dungeon" or "play" room, the inside of a living body, and the mysterious zones opened or crossed by shamans and other adepts, including leathermen. Mains depicts various *play spaces*. Some are semipublic, like the cubicles at the Slot or the Catacombs' large backroom. Others are private dungeons in homes, lit by gas flames, adorned with specialized fixtures, filled by the beats from subwoofers. Like the Lesser and Greater mysteries of Eleusis, leather space both mirrors and directs a sequence of illumination. The events are cut off from daily reality. They reverberate to their own rhythms—sometimes enthusiastic drumming, more often recorded music sequenced to encourage alterations of mind. "There is little room for distraction, frill, or fancy music" (*UA*, 106). Mains enumerates classical composers for one private scene (37). Gayle Rubin describes an evening's music at the Catacombs moving from "high-energy, sexually suggestive disco" to "moodier, darker, and sometimes menacing electronic music."[7]

The rhythms drive participants *inward*. Like Christian *askêsis*, leather "play" names both bodily discipline and spiritual warfare. For Mains, it charts and then recharts bodily terrains to find ways into spirit. Barriers, boundaries, frontiers, limits are multiplied then breached: pleasure and pain, acceptable and forbidden, skin and psyche, life and death.[8] Bondage immobilizes the body to focus attention within. Fisting is an excursion into disowned anatomy.

When Mains speaks of "new terrains and pleasures," he almost quotes Foucault's wistful irony at the end of *History of Sexuality*, volume 1: "someday, perhaps, in another economy of bodies and pleasures."[9] In Mains, that day is now.

For all the emphasis on the body, the more important space for *Urban Aboriginals* is consciousness, "head space." This space expands into another, much harder to describe. Sometimes Mains evokes it with images borrowed from the comparative study of *mysticism*: His "large, hazy ocean of sensation" sounds like the "oceanic" experience that Romain Rolland described to Freud as "spontaneous religious feeling."[10] Again, "leather is a sub-culture . . . [of] a purification by constant shattering" (*UA*, 33). Many "Christian mystics" would recognize that description, if not all the means recommended for attaining it. Main does not shatter his own language when trying to describe these ultimate spaces, but he does mark his narrative distance from them. *Urban Aboriginals* tells the most intense experiences in the third person. This may be an effort at self-protection, but it also suggests a transition or trajectory that splits the self. Some transformations produced by leather rituals just cannot be reported by the person who enters them or returns to the ordinary.

I will not guess how many readers are scandalized by the activities that Mains describes. (They are surely fewer than those who pretend to be shocked.) If there is scandal in *Urban Aboriginals*, it may be the risk of publishing esoteric knowledge, circulating secrets disclosed in guarded rituals. The serviceable prose in which Mains writes many of his narratives and all of his scientific explanations is an odd vessel for scalding insight. If you believe that leather rites are "aboriginal" in the sense Mains means, then you may be obliged to protect them with shamanic distortions. If these are unspeakable mysteries ("the unrepeatables," in the

Eleusinian idiom), they should not be spoken to the uniniti-
ated—and perhaps cannot be. Again, speaking so plainly
Mains may contradict one of the first lessons in Carlos
Castañeda: "To any beginner . . . the knowledge of sorcery
was rendered incomprehensible by the outlandish characteristics of the phenomena he [or she or they] experienced."[11]
Rendered incomprehensible: The ethical obligation to protect secrets is doubled or enforced by their outlandish character. Of course, and despite the appearances, Mains may be
a more cunning writer than the plainness of his text suggests.
The juxtaposed languages in *Urban Aboriginals*, its honey-
comb of spaces, its layering of religious analogies—these
devices keep secrets while restaging a beginner's incredulity
at what bodies can learn.

Ecstasy's Genders

While Mains talks of men throughout, he notices from time
to time that women also appeared at the Catacombs. He
mentions new organizations for leather women and the
writings that they produce, including the anthology *Coming
to Power*, assembled by the San Francisco collective SAM-
OIS and published originally in 1981.

Coming to Power provides an interesting contrast with
Urban Aboriginals on questions of spirituality. One of the
anthology's contributors, "Juicy Lucy," lists "exorcism" and
"spiritual" among the attributes of lesbian S/M. She notes
immediately that other lesbians would disagree. Disagreement does not keep her from using spiritual language: "The
spirit provides, & she brought me a confrontation with sexual S/M & my own self," "I feel myself open psychically so
much I could take in the whole universe & I can feel spirit
enter me like a lover," "S/M is about . . . our right to work with
our sacred life's energy as intensely creatively & courageously

as we wish." For Lucy, spirit's gender is clear: "I celebrate the female principle, the creatrix spirit." Her piece ends with a benediction: "Spirit surround you."[12]

Other writers in *Coming to Power* figure the divine. "I am her Goddess," says one player in a distant scene.[13] Another piece quotes Chaucer's wife of Bath, attributing her ethical insight to the Goddess. Still, by comparison with *Urban Aboriginals*, the authors of the SAMOIS anthology invoke spirit rarely and magic almost never. There are other books by women about BDSM, of course. They mix terminology differently. But looking only at lesbian leather texts might give a false sense of continuity. For me, the salient question is not whether women speak as frequently of spirit as the men in Mains do. The question is what meaning particular women make when they use "spirit," "ritual," "goddess." The similarity of leather practice, especially in shared spaces, might lead a reader to assume that the meaning of the terms was also stable. I hope to turn that assumption into a question.

I typically do this by provocative juxtaposition—which is more interesting than assigning a perfunctory "compare and contrast." For several years, I tried to add here narratives from women's music festivals. I was drawn to the most famous: the Michigan Womyn's Music Festival, held first in 1976 and last in 2015. (The Catacombs opened in 1975 and closed for a final time in 1984.) Each of the Festival's forty summers was different: The schedule varied from year to year along with the camping arrangements, the food, quarrels over rules, weather. Each "event" refracted into thousands of bodily itineraries, set by choices about when to listen, dance, sleep, or play. This was an immediate block to writing: I was beginning with an aggregate event rather than a set of texts. Any adequate retelling of one of the gatherings, especially by an outsider, would risk blurring together individual accounts—or falling back on institutional archives—to produce an "average" experience. I do not credit calculations of average experience. My pursuit of queer bodily arts depends on individual efforts to adapt or create language. It also requires that I be able to inhabit some part of the emerging language as a way of life. But I never attempted to attend MichFest, even when I lived not far away. The attempt would have been disrespectful. It would also have been refused.

This was the more interesting block. Here is the reasoning behind my exclusion in the homemade brochure that announced the 1977 gathering: "The political basis of the festival is the creation and affirmation of women's space. We feel it essential that women can come together to learn through music and through collective sharing of our cultures, skills and energies."[14] Adult men were not allowed to enter or remain. Male children posed a continuing problem. There were also notorious and divisive controversies over trans inclusion. I will not endorse or litigate the reasoning behind my own exclusion. I also do not want to mislead you about my physical presence in other settings I describe. On many pages of this book, I rely on texts to write about places where I never put my body. That is what I started to do with MichFest, too. Over several years, I gathered numerous texts about it. I listened to affecting tales of interventions by the Goddess during the festival—conversions, ecstasies, smaller boons. I made playlists based on musical performances during particular festival nights. I stirred my own memories of sensations from that Michigan landscape. But I was blocked by the spiritual implications of gender separatism.

The implications are more perplexing than the privacy of a sex club like the Catacombs. According to the official account, the Land in Michigan is, for the duration of the festival, separated and separatist. It is marked off on other principles than the leather spaces described by Mains. Sexual scenes and other rituals take place within the Festival's seclusion, of course, but the boundary around the large event is at once political, biological, and cosmic. The men (and then women) invited to the Catacombs are not (or not yet) different kinds of human beings than those who are not invited. If (mostly male) leatherspace grants insights and performs therapies not available elsewhere, it does not begin its transformation from a difference in being. The demarcation between leathermen and other men is not considered ontological (to import a philosopher's unhandy word). By contrast, the border of the Land at MichFest is supposed to depict and enforce ontology. No, the border says, we are not all "human beings" (as patriarchy constitutes that category). I can never quite grasp the assumptions behind that declaration, but I certainly feel their force. They differ evidently from any sorting by "sexual identity." To judge from the Festival's controversies over trans inclusion, they also supersede "gender identity." I am excluded from the language(s) of MichFest by my (assigned, morphological, essentialized) masculinity. Do I actually have that? I doubt it. Or, if I do, not adequately enough to convince some very loud men. But the separatist boundary makes me aware that I take up a different relation to the words "woman" and "man."

My exclusion from MichFest does not prevent me from admiring in it the ardent pursuit of queer bodily disciplines. Their scope reaches as far as the lesbian/feminist effort to rediscover or remake a free female body. I am reminded of an early feminist pamphlet. In *Women and Their Bodies* (1970), a picture of two women tilling a field dressed only in briefs illustrates a paragraph that reads: "Sex has got to do with the body—that alien part of us residing below the neck that has needs and responses that we don't understand. But all our feelings reside in the body."[15] A body that may play in a tent or forest clearing after a festival night's last musical set can also learn skills for setting up sound gear. A skilled body is not only a sexual body, but sex is a bodily skill—and a ritual one.

Unable and unwilling to cross the boundary around MichFest, I finally remembered that I had close to hand another example of speech on bodily arts in separatist spirituality. Close to hand, because I am a dedicated reader of lesbian separatist science fiction and its sister genres. There are many vivid examples from which to choose, but I return to one of the books that introduced me to the rest: Sally Gearhart's *Wanderground: Tales of the Hill Women* (1978).[16] This is the same Sally Gearhart who appeared earlier as coeditor of the anthology *Loving Women / Loving Men: Gay Liberation and the Church* (1974). If her role in the anthology was disruptive, her novel is stronger still.

Wanderground describes a community of lesbian separatists who are trying to heal the earth after it has been poisoned by patriarchy. Men still inhabit the ailing planet, but most of them are trapped in decaying, totalitarian cities. Neither their machines nor their penises function properly in the wild. A few other men, "gentles" or "unmanly men," live both in the cities and outside them. They "[touch] no women at all" because they recognize that male touch is inherently violent. While in the cities, they may have male lovers; outside, they seem grateful for impotence (2, 158, 168, 172). Note, here again, that dichotomous bodily gender supersedes sexual orientation or claimed identity. The "essential fundamental knowledge" of gender is that "women and men cannot yet, maybe not ever, love one another without violence; they are no longer of the same species" (152). I am grateful for that "maybe."

Gearhart projects separatism through religion into spirit. Her mentions of Christianity are divided into female and male, peaceful and violent. There were once "vigilante Christian groups who patrolled the parks with clubs looking for queers." "People, particularly religious fanatics, were outraged against the women." Yet "Lesbian Priest" appears in a flashback of headlines illustrating women's progress (111, 200, 185). Christian terms have also been carried over into the Wanderground's language, though their original meaning is forgotten: "This was the grace-making, the creation of extra attention and love, either toward one woman or toward a number of them. Zephyr did not understand what *grace* meant: it was now an archaic word." Archaic and yet unforgettable. So too are some church institutions. The women's central council turns out to be a "Long Dozen," members of an apostolic college (157, 160).

For me, the explicit or implicit references to (a) religion are less persuasively hopeful than the book's descriptions, page after page, of new arts for bodies. Many require psychic abilities: telepathy, clairvoyance, teleportation, levitation. The book often reminds the reader that skills like these will have to be learned, after gender separation, alongside farming that respects the earth, house-making for variable family configurations, guarding land that is not an empire, and giving birth without male violence. Gearhart invents words to describe each of these. But she also blurs demarcations between prose and poetry—between routine social exchanges and high hymn. There are many forms of worship on the Wanderground, mostly inseparable from the fullness of daily life. In one of the book's most distinctive rites, a woman heals from what befell her in the man-city by singing a poetic remaking of the myth of Kore. In her song, Kore is forced to change from male to female. (Note this transition at the center of a separatist hymn.) Kore then becomes a model of women's friendship as antidote to male sexual violence. You might object that the rewriting is didactic politics. But the song tells most the styling of queer bodies through subtle arts.

Bodies Learn Languages

I rehearse words that some writers used for the skills or arts needed to inhabit queer bodies. Doing that, I break rules built into a scheme of sexual identities. Among its many functions, the scheme regulates who gets to speak or write on specified topics. In some situations, at least, it grants first-person testimonies unique authority, especially when "coming out." A lesbian can be invited to respond to any question from the lesbian point of view, while a gay man inevitably gives a gay perspective. (This is still the recipe for too many public panels.) It should go without saying that there is no single lesbian point of view or (God knows) any single gay perspective. Indeed, there is no fixed lesbian or gay "experience" that allows one member to speak for all others in the alleged class. Is it good to hear a range of voices, especially on sexual questions? Yes, and the more the better! But you do not respect the range of experiences when you require one to speak (and to speak only) as spokesperson for many.

I go further. Our scheme of identities assumes not only that one can speak for many but that one can speak reliably for oneself. It enshrines language as coerced generalization. An invitation to speak my experience is the demand that I generalize it to render it recognizable. No experience can enter language (or be counted as "experience") except through risky negotiations with ill-fitting words. Our mother tongue is our first inheritance. It is also an obligation to ongoing cultural appropriation. I must speak—first, mostly— through what I have *not* made. My daily appropriation of a "mother tongue" is simultaneously its appropriation of my body, not least when it constitutes me as a speaker. Language describes and deputizes me through its words.

In the Catacombs, on the Land, across the Wanderground, body arts are used to pry open inherited speech wide enough to reshape a portion of it. Settled languages can be broken by intense sensation and emotion but also through *askêsis* and epiphany. Under certain artful disciplines, the body that will later speak is loosed a little from its linguistic bondage. It moves otherwise—and so prepares to speak otherwise. Learning a language is bodily training. Other bodily training may suggest or demand different categories or noises. Readers of texts expect sometimes to encounter the phrase "Words fail me." They may pause. They may even stop when a text compels them to do so—because *it* breaks up, garbles meaning, shifts to strange language, groans or whimpers, lapses into silence. Still, most readers do not stop long enough when they encounter the labor of languages in the vicinity of sex. Let me say it: Words fail. They must if we are to live sex otherwise. They fail more when we wish sex to remain familiarly the same.

Queer archives can expand memory and enrich language. But misread, mishandled, they homogenize memory and dehydrate language. The familiarity of a few erotic terms and plots deceives us into supposing that there is more than enough room for saying whatever we need to say about sex. It even suggests that everything has already been said. Every coming-out story is a cliché before it begins, not least because it is heard as another instance of a deliberately restrictive genre. A trivializing presumption of familiarity is the ridiculous pretense that the labor of queer language has already been accomplished—once and for all. In fact, it had barely begun before it was smothered by epidemic disaster and converted into sitcom plots and luxury styles.

Here is a hesitant story about an individual body. Its plot, setting, and incidents will sound clichéd. Resist the reflex to dismiss it as always already familiar. Listen to it not for biographical disclosures (hardly worth your while) but for the creaking, snapping, groaning of recently minted queer terms and their plots. Listen to it mostly as one story about learning a little queer language through a middle-aged body. This account of a familiar step in "coming out," over which I have labored, is inadequate to the bodily discoveries it pretends to register. Read the account for what it fails to do.

On a July 4 many years ago, I joined the queer celebration at the local dance club. I was in South Bend, Indiana, home of the Fighting Irish of Notre Dame and my home for too many years. The Land of MichFest was about 160 miles due north along US-31. That night, my attention settled on a young man whom I will call the Angel—not because he appeared a divine messenger (he may have been) but because of the way he spread his arms like wings when dancing. He wore baggy, unremarkable clothes over an average body. He was not "hot," and I was not "cruising." An unpromising student, I was trying to learn the ritual before me. He danced by himself in a country where (I had been taught) men are supposed to dance only when lured onto the floor by women.

The Angel kept his head down. His weight settled into his hips. His feet were planted together (in rawhide hiking boots, white socks folded over the tops—historians of club style, note well). For a moment, a minute, he was stubbornly still in the middle of the hops, jumps, spins of the other dancers. As if he didn't hear the music or could not yield to it. Then one of his feet began to tap the main beat. With a swerve of the hips, his arms shot up for the first time. Like wings or the outstretched arms of a vested celebrant at a Eucharistic altar. The Angel danced with his hips, his arms, his head, but he would not move his feet except to beat time. No steps, slides, or turns. Just the shaking count that moved up through his torso and out into blessing.

I did not know that you could name that "dancing."

I did not know how to "dance" like that.

I did feel and perhaps could almost begin to describe a promise of bodily art.

In some accounts of lives later called queer, people describe feeling as if they were the only ones in the world to be swept by certain desires. Others admit to doing things without knowing that the acts constituted "homosexuality," which they had heard condemned so gruesomely. Still others assume that same-sex acts are harmless since the only moral warnings they had received concerned the "opposite sex."

On that South Bend night, a certain version of "house music" was still in full possession of gay dance floors. I later learned to name Blackbox's "Strike It Up" or C & C Music Factory's "Gonna Make You Sweat (Everybody Dance Now)." I was drawn into fans' disputes about the origins of house (Chicago, New York?), its founders, its denominations. No need to rehearse them now. For the moment, I underline just one thing: House is often explicit about its ritual power—and not only because it copies soprano lines from Black Gospel. House summons you to the dance floor to rededicate your body. It is an "altar call," an appeal to step forward in surrender. Let the weight go, hand over the burden, and then—fly, soar, sing all the way to heaven. The soloist—the diva—screams in ecstatic rage against the unyielding beat. "You cannot hold me down." "You cannot bind me." "I will no longer abide your proprieties." "I will not crouch within the denial that you demand." For that matter, I will no longer inhabit assigned identities.

Years later, I learned to say that I most like to dance to or under "ambient techno" (blessings on your head, *Artificial*

Intelligence and Aphex Twin). I was also listening to "mini-malist" composers. What was happening to my musical taste, I sometimes wondered? David Toop explained. I had not fallen far from Debussy's "open, intuitive, impressionis-tic soundworld." On dance floors, too, I chased music that opened "impossible, imaginary landscapes of beauty and terror," "music that searches for new relationships between maker and listener, maker and machine, sound and context," "a shifting zone . . . a mode of imaginal travel."[17] I wanted to offer my shamed body as a manuscript for the formulas of spiritual alchemy.

6

Pulp Poetics

Entering a shadowy bar or a dance club for the first time, rushing through the opening pages of a pulp novel, lining up for a protest, reaching a music festival or leather encampment—these arrivals are often described as the discovery of another world, unsuspected and always sought. A child's fantasy is fulfilled. You really were left behind to be raised by uncomprehending strangers. Now your true parents return to reclaim you—with a gypsy caravan, troupe of fairies, grand circus, team of alien explorers. These are my people! They speak my language—which I need only to brush up on. I recognize their customs and costumes, however dreamily. They will teach proficiency in my mother tongue, which anciently dedicated names for our kind.

One reply to this fantasy—I offer it tenderly—is that there are indeed groups of people gathered around their exclusion from the prescribed grammars of male-female attraction. The groups can have peculiar ways of talking. Joining their dialogues may give the thrill of acquiring speech that drops over your body like a signature perfume, that opens doors

onto rooms furnished just for you. Or that is what it feels like
for a while—perhaps a long while, if you have been very
badly treated before. Then, sooner or later, you realize that
even the delightful words do not fit exactly. The offered
furniture is still measured to another body's specifications.
You must remake the language as you try to learn it—because
you are learning it, with your soul and body. Your new
friends are not magical beings who have returned to teach
you the holy tongue. They too make it up as they go along.
Indeed, what they really have to offer is their craft of invention. Their world—this world—remains always and never
yours. Your Home is Neverland. You find your way there by
making stories about the journey. The yellow brick road is
actually paved with words.

I simplify the picture by describing languages learned
face to face. Often queer seekers find their way home with
the help of books. Some of the books might strike you as
unlikely guides. For decades, language-making for queer
lives has been carried out in the cluster of genres called
"science fiction," "fantasy," "speculative fiction," or other
things. Thousands of pages and postings argue proposed
definitions for these genres. With Octavia Butler, I find
myself mostly uninterested in the labels. "I write about
people who do extraordinary things. It just turned out that it
was called science fiction."[1]

People who do extraordinary things. For me, reading
science fiction started out as a safely obscure declaration of
deviance. As a boy, I found in sci-fi novels a gallery of "queer"
lives. I would not have known to call them that, at least not
at first, but I studied the portrayals as intently as if they held
my secret. They did. During bleached Texas summers,
sprawled on a thin rug in the coolest room of my grand-
mother's house, I read my way onto exotic worlds where
people were allowed to be . . . queer (in an older sense,

which still carried exotic shame). Their lives had shapes not mentioned around her dinette table. Under wispy red suns or moons of ice, beside murmuring ruins of alien cities, men and women and people who were neither were transformed as they never could have been earthside—that is, in south Dallas. They unriddled strange religions. They endured monstrous visions that transformed them into gods. Often enough, they ended by preferring life out there, beyond terrestrial certainties, to life here. I could only agree.

Sometimes the strangeness moved closer to my reach. I remember the disbelieving thrill I felt, over the thrum of the window unit, when I realized that "André Norton" was the pen name of a woman. I knew from French class that "André" was "Andrew." How could a woman be an Andrew? And why had some of her novels been published originally under the name "Andrew North"? Somewhat later, I was stopped at the local branch library when I tried to check out Brian Aldiss's *Starship*. The librarian looked at me sourly while she explained that the book, now firmly in her hands, "talks about things that aren't for boys." My mother returned the next day to sign a form giving me permission to check out whatever I fancied—on the theory, I suppose, that reading any library book had to be beneficial. The embarrassing episode taught me that some sci-fi, like dirty words and pictures of naked bodies, was restricted to adults. I set about finding it. I came to idolize Alfred Bester's *The Demolished Man*. I raced to the drugstore for copies of the sci-fi monthly *Analog*—causing my father to puzzle over my sudden interest in computation.

Somewhere along the way, I contracted academic ambitions and mostly put aside such childish things. During my senior year of college, I did commit myself to *Gravity's Rainbow* by Thomas Pynchon. No one could accuse me of reading mere science fiction when I carted around that

labyrinth of a text. A year later, in my first semester of graduate school, a classmate joked that if I could make my way
through Pynchon, I could probably also endure a "massive"
new novel, Samuel Delany's *Dhalgren*. I bought it that Sat-
urday and added it to the stack beside my bed. A few weeks
later, I sat up in bed when I reached the scene, not too many
pages into the mass, when the Kid gets a blowjob from Tak.
Men with men: Here was my desire right at a novel's surface.
Men remaking themselves and each other through erotic
liturgies in the ruins of a city. I did not understand that the
fantastic landscape was an image of gay life in Manhattan,
where fiery rockets lit up the moonless nights of back
rooms, warehouses, baths. *Dhalgren* was Delany's Green-
wich Village—and *Dhalgren* was my private dream.

Language can migrate, conquering new territory to transform unexpected bodies. What original cast albums of
Broadway musicals were for some queer boys, sci-fi paper-
backs were for others. Costumes, colored lights, unexpected
music, painted faces, the sweep of exotic geographies—it
could be Oklahoma or Aldebaran. If genders bent under
greasepaint, they multiplied or vanished on other worlds.
Light years from suburban shopping centers that smelled of
overheated engines and melting tar, strange creatures of
reverie danced across pulp pages. Delany himself has com-
plained that the "freedom" of science fiction meant for its
writers poor pay, shoddy business practices, and lack of recognition.[2] Still, it was a sort of freedom, especially for the
shared imagination of sexes and genders. Some days, I still
find myself wishing that I had come out as a Venusian.

I return now to Delany's capacious "science fiction" narratives in part because they emphasize variations of sex or
gender, in part because they are so thoroughly imagined. But
I also return because language is his constant preoccupation.
He reminds us—by confecting so many alternatives—how

much of the official language for condemning desires has also been "science fiction," in a more aggressive and tedious sense. The sodomite, the invert, the homosexual, the lesbian or the gay man: These are characters in science-fiction plots. We accept the imposition of such fantastically alien vocabularies under the authority of science become theology. Why not from sources more congenial to our ways of life?

Delany: Language on Triton

Another novel by Delany appeared while I was in graduate school: *Triton*, subtitled *An Ambiguous Heterotopia*.[3] On Delany's version of the satellite world, there are "forty or fifty basic sexes, falling loosely into nine categories, [of which] four [are] homophilic" (99). "Homophilic" refers not to the genital anatomy of your preferred partners but to those with whom you choose to live. Marriage is illegal—not just for couples of like genitals but for everyone. The satellite's ambient sexual ethics prizes toleration, variety, and revocable consent. Individuals can change race, gender, sex, and sexual preference at will through state-subsidized medical interventions. In short, Triton is a queer utopia—if by "queer" you mean practicable affirmation of the greatest fluidity in sex/gender configurations. For those whose type of queerness still requires the whiff of transgression, Triton even offers an "unlicensed sector."

Delany does not regard Triton as any kind of *utopia*. The novel's protagonist, Bron, who begins it as a man and ends it as a woman, grapples with the array of social choices to pursue desolation. A thoroughly unreliable narrator, he-then-she is also an uncongenial narcissist who slips, by the novel's last sentence, into uncomprehending despair. (On Triton, the system of English pronouns has not been altered: Medical transitions are represented as shifts between binary pronouns.) The protagonist shows that some selves can change planets, sociopolitical regimes, and sexes while remaining jerks—I mean, while avoiding the ethical challenge of fashioning an adult self. The narrator's persistent refusal to grow contests the fantasy that sexual revolution is achieved just by swapping identities.

Against the boorish narrator, Delany puts the figure of Ashima Slade. Modeled after Wittgenstein, Slade has discovered or invented "metalogics," the basis of Triton's knowledge economy. Though immensely wealthy, Slade—like Wittgenstein—lives in austere isolation, sharing obscure remarks on his current thinking with a knot of students. Slade—like Wittgenstein—is associated through a group called the "Circle" with other logicians, poets, and musicians. And Slade—like Wittgenstein—has a partly secret history of sex and gender. It is not clear whether Slade—like Wittgenstein—suffered accusations of indefensible attractions to students.

Since Triton is Triton, Slade's history is rather more vivid than Wittgenstein's. Born a man on Mars, Slade immigrates to the satellites at seventeen and soon after becomes a woman. Through a chance meeting with a poet, she is led to enroll in the university. At twenty, she publishes the first volume of the *Summa of Metalogics*. Slade then becomes deeply involved with the artists of the Circle. Twenty years later, Slade joins a few of them and some religious practitioners to form a commune. The commune lasts exactly three months before collapsing violently. Slade is found blind on the streets, suffering from self-inflicted wounds—and having become again male. After his commune's violent dispersal, Slade moves in as a permanent guest of the Sygn, a sect vowed to silence and chastity.

Delany's *Triton* offers a nonclichéd way of conceiving the connections between literature and queer self-making. On that moon, the queer is the stylized resolution to wager one's lifetime on the torsion—the twist—between any fixed categories and the art of a sexed life. Bron's impulsive attempt to redeem a failing self by assuming another, all-too-literal gender is not queer. Neither is same-sex desire or polyamorous communes or polymorphous perversity. On Triton, queer life is lived emblematically in Ashima Slade's final cell, in the half-solitude between perpetually excavated speech and silence, in a body that is the palimpsest—the overwritten manuscript—of something that cannot be fixed with a name.

The novel's appendix recounts Slade's death and gestures toward his final thinking. It is written as a scholarly article with extensive quotations from Slade's working papers. (The satire of academic style is apt if ambivalent.) The article opens with a quotation from Foucault on languages in utopias and heterotopias. According to this Foucault, utopia is an imaginary place that cannot exist on this earth, "'a fantastic, untroubled region . . . with vast avenues, superbly planted gardens'" (292).[4] It is *u-topia*, no-place. By contrast, a heterotopia (Foucault borrows an anatomical term) is a real place, set aside by an existing society, in which basic social relations can be represented, contested, and inverted. It is an "outside" permitted into the city—under continuing surveillance. (Call to mind sex-work districts or lesbian and gay neighborhoods before their gentrification.) Delany quotes more of Foucault on how heterotopias bend language: "They make it impossible to name this and that . . . they shatter or tangle common names . . . they destroy 'syntax' in advance, and not only the syntax with which we construct sentences but also that less apparent syntax which causes words and things (next to and also opposite one another) to 'hold together'" (292). For Ashima Slade, to be queer depends on dwelling in heterotopias that elicit heteroglossia—in

other places that call for other speech. (I adapt a literary
term from translations of Bakhtin.) On Triton, the queerest
character is a poet-logician. The queerest copulation, sex as
unending evasion of literal certainty.

Ashima Slade is killed just as he begins a long-awaited
lecture series. His death is accidental or impersonal: It
results from an act of war that kills five million people. Slade
is interrupted mid-speech before an audience that watches
through holographic streaming. He had announced the
lecture series under three headings: shadows, objectives,
illuminations. (Compare, among many other possible sources,
Plato's *Republic* 509d–511e .) In the last lecture, particularly,
Slade might have returned to one of his characteristic styles,
"richly condensed (if not impenetrable) metaphor . . . more
reminiscent of the religious mystic than the philosopher of
logic" (295–96). There are samples from the notes for the
first lecture, the one interrupted by massacre. For example,
"There is no class, race, nationality or sex that it does not
help to be only half" (301).

Slade is a more vivid Wittgenstein, but Slade is also Tiresias, the blind seer, favored and cursed by the gods, who can
arbitrate sexual pleasures across gender—and who becomes,
for modernist literature, the figure of spirit after established
religion.[5] The evocation of Tiresias reminds us to search on
Triton for other gods. Slade's final cell is offered to him by
the Sygn, one of many religious groups on Triton. Across its
first pages, the novel mentions the Poor Children of the
Avestal Light and the Changing Secret Name—that is one
group—but also the Rampant Order of Dumb Beasts,
"another neo-Thomist sect" vowed to abolishing meaning-
less communication (2, 12). If it is hard for Bron, the protagonist, to keep track of Christian revivals, Delany's references
might still deserve another minute's attention. Wittgenstein
is everywhere in *Triton*, but Thomas Aquinas appears as

well—not least in the title of Slade's masterwork, another *Summa*. Thomas is often (if inaccurately) associated with the ideal of a grand "Scholastic synthesis." Perhaps that is what Delany has in mind with Slade's *Summa*. But Thomas begins his *Summa* with reminders that language must fail radically when it tries to speak the divine. His teaching on "divine names" (recall Delany's "Poor Children") is a classic reiteration of negative or apophatic theology—of theology that insists on denying language when approaching God. There is no single God in Ashima Slade's *Summa* (or none that we hear of), but there is negation or apophasis. It applies to bodies that might—that must—be regarded as queer.

In Delany's novel, religious groups are obsessed with bodies at the boundaries of speech. That preoccupation ties them to other creativities in the unlicensed sector—to the street theater of the Circle and the house of the Sygn and the birth of metalogics. Just here the word "spiritual" makes its crucial appearances in the novel. In the novel's first significant scene, Bron decides to cut through the unlicensed sector on the way home from work. He becomes the unwitting spectator of an astonishing street performance—in which he not only gets to save a damsel supposedly in distress but to meet the woman who will obsess him. When he tracks her down again, Spike explains the performance's purpose: "'to experience a greater order than the quotidian can provide. A moment of verbal, spatial, and *spiritual* energy in resolution" (75, emphasis added). So that the word may not be overlooked, it is repeated two pages later—with reference to a homoerotic attraction. The female-identified Spike is narrating a time when she had her sexual desire clinically "refixated" onto women: "'There was a very marvelous woman once who was very fond of me, *spiritually* and sexually, and wanted me very badly" (77, emphasis added). Her desire redirected, Spike spent a happy season with this theatrical director.

Of course, you may be thinking, the appearance of the word "spiritual" in the context of a discussion of same-sex desire might be accidental. But there is one more use of the word that counts against that interpretation. It occurs in the biography—the hagiography—of Ashima Slade: "A great deal of personal, social, and *spiritual* interplay occurred between members of the Circle and members (and ex-members) of the Sygn" (163, emphasis added). The Sygn is the religious order that gives Ashima Slade shelter until the end of his life—after a final change of sex, while he continues to chip away at the foundations of language. The Circle is the group of artists to which Spike herself belonged. Put the pieces together. In *Triton*, "spirituality" refers to a level of "energy" beyond the "quotidian" that can fashion new beauties, invent languages, transform embodied subjects by performing relations from other places and times. A heterotopia disconnects words from things, rupturing the syntax that binds language to itself and its objects (so the quotation from Foucault). In the space of the rupture, language is refashioned by what is described as religious obsession or spirituality.

To say the obvious: "Spirituality" so understood names the work of Delany's own novel, with its prophecies of queer selves yet to arrive. Still, the prophecies come as descriptions of what happens offstage, beyond the novel's edge. There are Spike's performances: A short one is described in detail, but we cannot experience it fully without the aid of the psychotropic drug administered to the audience of one. About her masterpieces, the reader hears only snippets of praise. There are also the works of Ashima Slade: the meta-logic, which *Triton* never attempts to describe; and the lectures, which are cut short by carnage. Delany puts forward characters who have witnessed what he cannot see or say.

Delany: Poets of the Future

Poets and poetry appear regularly in Delany's novels. The poets are often women who are both political actors and teachers of language. An obvious example: The protagonist of *Stars in My Pocket Like Grains of Sand* passes from a mute pidgin to full fluency by absorbing women's poetry directly with the help of advanced technology. His poetic education becomes a joke for the cosmopolitan woman who has purchased him for his body.

I concentrate on the figures of poets or poetry in two earlier novels by Delany, both published before *Triton*. The first, *Empire Star*, appeared as an "Ace Double" along with his *Ballad of Beta-2*.[6] (Delany had wanted it bound with *Babel-17*.) He had a personal connection with the publisher: His wife worked there. (About her, about them, more in due time.) The double publication was his first in book form. On its face, *Empire Star* is a galactic quest crosshatched by repetitions: It tells stories about the loops of storytelling in which everyone except the protagonist has heard all the stories before.

The story unfolds a slowly recognized fate. In repeated scenes, diction is taught, music played, terms explained, poems written, books recalled. Slaves, indispensable builders, are finally set free—or not. There is a supercomputer, a linguistic ubiquitous multiplex (or literary text), disguised as a jewel. The jewel narrates the story we read. (Imagine a 1960s sci-fi story told as Joyce's *Ulysses* or Musil's *The Man without Qualities*.) A mad poet, Ni Ty Lee, versifies events as they happen. Together, the poet and the jewel recite a litany of literary names to explain the sentimental education of writers: Oscar Wilde and Alfred Douglas, Paul Verlaine and Arthur Rimbaud . . . (remember, this is a gimmick-paperback pulp novella). Ni Ty's own mentor was one Muels Aranlyde (an anagram of Samuel R. Delany). Aranlyde has written a political trilogy that supplies, not coincidentally, the larger frame for the present story. The story follows Comet Jo, a "beautiful boy" who must finally be understood as the Reader, otherwise referred to as "she" (32, 89). In the final sentence, she is told to order her perceptions and then make "the journey from one to the other" (92). One perception to another, one state of consciousness to another, one language to another, one gender to another? End of the first novella.

Babel-17 was originally published as part of another "Ace Double" in 1966. At first glance, there is little to distinguish it from other space operettas of that year. Certainly not the cover by Jerome Podwil: Against a background of tarnished avocado, it depicts a construction crane, a silver robot, a generically "Asian" young woman of a type produced by Las Vegas, and the close-up of a menacing eye encircled by planets. The tagline: "Think galactic—or your world is lost!" Much of Delany's plot is also operatic: hidden schemes, exotic customs, secret technology, and an improbable romance right at the happy ending—which throws open the door for a sequel. Wrapped in this garish covering, there is the surprise of queer thinking about language, self, and desire.

The protagonist is Rydra Wong, a poet who enjoys something approaching galactic fame. Raised by parents who were experts in communication and translation, endowed by trauma with total verbal recall, she has abandoned military cryptography to write poetry. "I listen to other people, stumbling about with their half thoughts and half sentences and their clumsy feelings that they can't express—and it hurts me. So I go home and burnish it and polish it and weld it to a rhythmic frame . . . that's my poem" (18). Read that again as a description of the effort to make a queer language after centuries of enforced silence or punishing literalism.

Wong is recruited to decipher what military intelligence regards as a code. They call it Babel-17. She has already discovered that it is a completely new language. Somewhat later, she tries to summarize it for her crew (because she is also, of course, a starship captain): "Most of its words carry more information about the things they refer to than any four or five languages I know put together—and in less space" (69). So, for example, describing a restraining net in Babel-17 tells you how to break out of it. Such a language might also serve to escape a closet. Because this *is* a space operetta, the alien language is explained in terms of formal logic and with mathematical examples—as if it were only the idiom of engineers. But Babel-17 is also poetry, that is, language stripped to reveal its original energies.

What about the world depicted in *Babel-17* might count as queer—or at least lesbian and gay, to use older language? There are examples on every side, some of them rather bold within the default straightness of mid-1960s pulp science fiction.[7] For example, space ships are piloted by threesomes: "a triple, a close, precarious, emotional and sexual relation with two other people" (43). The triple we learn most about consists of two men and one woman. (The obligatory threesome of straight male fantasy is, of course, two women at the disposal of one man.) Perhaps that is why a customs officer mutters, "Perverts!" When Rydra Wong finds a third member for a triplet of navigators that has been broken by death, she chooses someone who does not yet speak English: a woman from Pan Africa who speaks Kiswahili. They will become a triple by teaching one another language.

Delany and Hacker, Hacker and Delany

In a note before the text of *Babel-17*, Delany explains that "all epigraphs . . . are from the poems of Marilyn Hacker." The poetic excerpts are published with the titles Hacker actually gave them. They are given more or less in Hacker's versions, though there are variations from the texts as finally printed.[8] In the novel, of course, the lines must be read as the verses of Rydra Wong, which the reader does not otherwise hear.[9] Marilyn Hacker gives voice to Rydra Wong, the poet who is Delany's hero.

Though frequently separated, Samuel Delany and Marilyn Hacker were married for almost twenty years (1961–1980). In potted biographies, this is described as the marriage between an always "homosexual" man, then nineteen, and a later lesbian woman, eighteen, who was unexpectedly pregnant. Delany gives his own account in memoirs and published journals. There are more austere hints in Hacker's poetry. I will not add to the explanations of why they got married, how they conducted their separate sex lives while spouses, or why they finally divorced. I keep the obvious labels and overdetermined plots away from them to hear how they make languages, together and apart. Two gifted writers learn each other's bodies, share work, and then present, separately, unabashed songs to desires not for each other. Around their bodies, between them, they improvise a baroque frankness for queer love, unabashed and formally constrained, sweating and lucid.

For *Babel-17*, Delany borrowed from Hacker more than the lines of the sections' epigraphs. Some ideas about the alien language were a shared effort, begun on the way back from a disastrous camping trip. Delany and Hacker wanted to invent a language from scratch. Its reformed syntax and vocabulary are what you might expect from precocious graduates of a high school famous for science. There are, for example, efforts to regularize relative prepositions, to use syntactic position more consistently, and so on. Still, whenever Delany describes the language game he played with Hacker, he emphasizes compactness. "It is very compact; it takes only half as much space to write."[10] Compression is also the chief character of the imagined language Babel-17.

There are other biographical connections, including (variable) triplets living in the disapproved neighborhoods of sexualized minorities. But, for me, the more interesting resonances between Delany and Hacker arise from their both writing between structuring form and unruly body.

Hacker: Diction of Wet Desire

Most introductions to Hacker's poetry begin by commenting on her dedication to traditional forms. An early poem she presented to Auden was a sestina—or almost, as Auden pointed out when he came to dinner at the apartment she shared with Delany.[11] Her first two collections contain poems named after their forms: sestina, villanelle, sonnet. At the same time, the poems excerpt "popular culture" and daily speech. There is an "Elegy (for Janis Joplin)" and, elsewhere, quotations from Joplin's songs.[12] The poetic play of structure and sensation is also a theme in many of Hacker's early poems. She attends, for example, to "the living figure in the windowpane." Touch, smell, silence are languages, "as real as any other" (*FC*, 7, 6).

In Hacker's first three books of poetry, before her divorce from Delany, explicit references to erotic loves between women are both uncommon and veiled. I cannot find unambiguous mentions before *Taking Notice* (published in 1980). Earlier verse leaves genders unspecified or mixed. Hacker's extended declaration of desire for women is *Love, Death, and the Changing of the Seasons* (1988), published about a decade after the novels by Delany I have considered. In a sequence of linked poems, Hacker narrates the year of her love for and with one of her writing students, Rachel (Rae, Ray). Some would make their relationship's origin into a charge against Hacker. Let me note, then, that in the course of the year Hacker turned forty and her student twenty-five. Hacker's own ethical sensitivity turns more to the difference in age than the power dynamics of the classroom setting. One of the book's two epigraphs is Shakespeare's Sonnet 73, "That time of year thou mayst in me behold. . . ."[13] Hacker also frets about her responsibility for Rachel's infidelity, since the younger woman is in another relationship when they first meet.

Poems are gifts between lovers and those who still hope for returned love. (A thin volume of Cavafy can be a voluble proposition.) More: Reading poetry together is notoriously seductive. (In Dante's *Inferno*, the emblematic lovers Paolo and Francesca fall into the sin of lust over a romance of Lancelot and Guinevere.) Hacker meets Rachel in a poetry seminar. Many of the poems that ensue are addressed to the younger woman, and the whole collection is dedicated to her indirectly, without naming her. The course of their love is marked by such communications and miscommunications: quarrels (of course), letters lost, scratchy phone calls across the Atlantic, and always Hacker trying to say what Rachel will not hear—or Hacker uncomprehending before messages transmitted in Rachel's code.

By the time the poems are published, the relationship has ended. Hacker declares herself resigned to the loss. The last poems in the cycle are aching depictions of grief accepted. One of them describes a lunch partner chiding her for not doing more to act out, fight back (*LD*, 211). Of course, the book is the cry, the calling out, even the effort to seduce again. Here, take this book of poems, a gift and accusation, an *envoi* and a plea for your return.

Across the year of pages, the bodies speak most power-fully—to each other and to the reader. Hacker's intricate patterns enclose pulses, touches, rubs, moans, cries. Mouths kiss or lick more than they talk. In 1894, Pierre Louÿs had published *The Songs of Bilitis*, scandalous for its depictions of lesbian love. Louÿs claimed to have translated them from Greek inscriptions discovered in circumstances worthy of Indiana Jones. In fact, he contrived the poems from earlier materials—a clever pseudonymy. In Hacker, the languid, wispy images of bodies that illustrate the *Songs* are replaced by mortal flesh. Women's bodies have freckles, hair, nipples, saliva, liquid salt. They know the pleasures of tongues and fingers, the delicious constraint of another's weight, how muscles go taut until abruptly loosened.

Hacker's gift for incorporating vernaculars completes itself in this book. Within the artful meters, rhymes, cross-references, and allusions, the poems talk dirty. They relish sexual words: "come," "cunt," "clit," "crotch." Phrases: "cream my jeans," "go down," "get laid." Even the patois of lesbian and gay life: "bitch," "butch," "dyke," "fag," "girls" and "boys," "gay" and "queer" (as in "queer girls"). Hacker cites pop music: the Shirelles, Simon and Garfunkel, Joni Mitchell, Cyndi Lauper (whose first hit, it should be remembered, was "Girls Just Wanna Have Fun"). Putting common words and current allusions into traditional forms is Hacker's most familiar art. She teaches the technique in her writing class, where "tight forms" force the students to "slang their diction down" (*LD*, 86). In these poems, something stronger happens. Hacker writes within traditional forms to contest the traditions that restricted them to approved topics. She makes love poetry out of words that were used to exclude her love. All the while, Hacker inscribes her text within the canon. She does it first of all by form. If that is not clear enough, she writes within and against "two thousand years of Western literature" by explicit citation (*LD*, 33). Here the reader will find Sappho, of course, but also Homer's *Iliad*, Dante's *Comedy*, Shakespeare (the sonnets, *Lear*), and canonical modernists like Verlaine, Rimbaud, or Pound. Hacker has sex with Rachel on the grassy slopes of Mount Parnassus.

There is not much explicitly religious reference in Hacker's *Love*, and its "spirituality" is the epiphany of sex itself—sex as itself, not as deputy for some higher truth. Still, one of the last poems in the cycle is "Letter on August 15." As Hacker makes plain, that day is the feast of the Assumption of Mary on current Roman Catholic calendars. For those who have forgotten their catechism or never had it incised: In her death-bed assumption (or dormition), Mary is raised bodily into heaven. At Vence, where Hacker finds herself, a feast is kept marking Mary's new mode of life in the body. Predictably, the poem is filled with religious references—Masses, candles lit for the dead, Hacker's own "hermitage." The lines lament the absence of sacraments that might explain the "unspecified contract" of the ring she still wears on her left hand (*LD*, 187). The "Letter" is a fruitless admonition to Rachel, a plea not to break the relationship by infidelity. By liturgical reckoning, the poem also anticipates Hacker's death through grief and the assumption of her body into—what? More life, of course, but also the new, the heavenly body of the book.

Hacker: Trembling Reticence

I have written these paragraphs on Hacker's poetry mocked in each sentence by the conviction that she has always already said it all better. (There is only one way to paraphrase a language like Babel-17: badly.) I have also felt the blush of transgressing yet another a prohibition—or, rather, two. The first prohibition tells me not to write about my body in desire—even if (or because?) Hacker writes so ardently about Rachel's body tangled with her own. The second warns me away from poetry, which is too high for me. The two are linked through the old anxiety of the "gay voice."

It ought to be safe for me to write as a scholar of sexuality about lesbian poetry—or, since that phrase is controversial, about a female poet writing out her bodily love for women.[14] I have been taught over decades how to comment on Hacker's book from a safe distance, apologizing now and then for intruding my male gaze, protesting just as often my lack of a license from the guild that claims to own poetic forms. But Hacker calls up in me more visceral anxieties of voice—of gendered pitch and affective timber, of rhythm that gives away too much. Hacker includes a delightful poem that begins "Do people look at me and know I'm gay?" (LD, 101–2). The poem is about walking down stairs and oral sex. I share its worries. Yet my more acute (aphasic, aphonic) reticence arises when there are words to be written or spoken.

In the modern English-speaking world, a fondness for poetry has sometimes been a dead giveaway, for adult men if not for women. Women were allowed to admire certain kinds of poetry and even to compose it without violating their gender norms. This indulgence would not have extended to Hacker's love poetry. Nor would it have countenanced the use of lesbian poetry readings for finding girlfriends. For men, the gendered suspicions would have been more comprehensive. Remember *Brideshead Revisited*: The one notoriously queer character, Anthony Blanche, recites lines from Eliot's "Waste Land" through a megaphone as the muscled crews row beneath him. He stands in for so many wan young men, the ones who clutch books of verse bound in lilac cloth or Moroccan leather and, in sadder years, carry uniform copies of A *Shropshire Lad* into the trenches. Alongside these literary clichés, there are the many examples of English verse by "gay" poets—anthologized at least since Anthony Reid's *Eternal Flame* and now made fully public, if not canonical. Or so we are assured.[15]

Hacker's *Love, Death* is the opposite of discrete. It makes room in the old poetic plots for the hot desires of unwelcome bodies. It also reserves an eloquent silence. In a decade when other lesbian-feminist poets reject the husks of a conserved erudition, Hacker writes her confession in full possession of them. She retains them to good effect. Much of the poetic cycle's force is the twist between the authorized topics or idioms and the poet's raw experience, the torsion between approved form and unexpected content. That tension, that torsion happens in the spaces around words, which is productive silence.

7

Sex Beyond

In arts for bodies and words, in asceticism of vision and verse, sexual desire has intertwined with spirit. If my texts have been chosen from the last fifty years or so, they belong to a much older genealogy of "spiritual" authors already established in English by the second half of the nineteenth century. The genealogy has not yet ended. Its writers preceded homophiles and liberationists. They have now outlasted them. Indeed, queer spiritual libraries remain a surprisingly active site for queer calling. A few years back, Mark Thompson wrote of the Radical Faeries, "We are the last of the original tribes to spring out of that heady brew concocted by late 1960s gay liberation, sexual revolution, civil rights, environmental concern and feminism."[1] I would say instead: The Faeries and their spiritual kin retain an older faith in politics by incantation.

Telling the rise and success of the movement for LGBT rights, publicists or textbook writers often omit the help given by established religious organizations. They focus instead on religion's oppressions—which were and are loud,

long, harmful. In the same way, the settled stories leave out
religious or spiritual motives within queer organizing. But
Harry Hay, who founded the Mattachine Society using an
idea sparked by reading Lenin, two decades later helped
convene the first national gathering of Faeries. Carl Wittman, who wrote the *Gay Manifesto* after service in radical
student politics and labor protests, left cities a few years later
to experiment with magic in the woodlands.

Hay and Wittman are hardly the only prominent activists
who combined movement politics with spiritual seeking.
Del Martin and Phyllis Lyon are rightly honored as leaders
of the Daughters of Bilitis; founders of the pioneering lesbian magazine, *The Ladder*; the most efficient organizers of
the Council on Religion and the Homosexual; and so courageously on. They were also full members of a New Thought
group, the Prosperos. The leader of the Prosperos, Thane-
Walker or Thane of Hawaii, claimed to have studied (perhaps at Fontainebleau?) with the Levantine wanderer
Gurdjieff, though there is a recognizably American lineage
as well.[2] He borrowed much besides the metaphysical view
of healing Mind: bits of clinical psychology or psychoanalysis; interests in astrology and paranormal phenomena; a
commitment to world transformation; and progressive con-
ceptions about sex, including same-sex relations.

Papers kept by Martin and Lyon contain many years of
publications from the Prosperos.[3] A report by Lyon about
Martin says that they met members of the Prosperos at the
Mattachine convention in Denver, which would be 1959.[4]
(The Prosperos and members of Mattachine had already
established contact in Los Angeles.) Lyon reports that Martin later faulted herself for being too ardent a convert and for
becoming preachy about the Prosperos' doctrine. Martin
caused some disagreement within the Daughters of Bilitis by
inviting Thane to address their annual meeting in 1962.[5] More

interesting to me are the detailed notes of Thane's classes in Lyon's careful hand. Their membership was not an empty formality. Nor was it one they were afraid to announce publicly, even in *Lesbian/Woman*: "As for ourselves, we are members of the Prosperos, a metaphysical group that offers spiritual enlightenment and a sense of being that has meaning for us."[6]

Alongside or entangled with New Thought lineages, there were a growing number of queer "neo-pagans" (another inadequate label). In a pamphlet derived from a 1974 talk to New York's Gay Liberation Front, John Lauritsen argues that the oppression of homosexuals, far from being natural, is a transient historical phenomenon that should be blamed on Judaism and especially Christianity.[7] Beyond the spheres of ancient Israel and its bloody stepchild the Christian Church, same-sex acts were happily linked to gods and heroes within nonoppressive fertility cults and temple worship. Perhaps that is why the pamphlet's cover illustration, entitled "Death of Pan," shows the horned, goatish deity staring from a hiding place at Christ's nativity.

A slightly later example, more fully developed, is Arthur Evans's *Witchcraft and the Gay Counterculture* (1978). This counterhistory of "Gay" people begins with an invocation to Isis, Diana, and Kali. It then claims for "Gay history" a diverse group of pre- or anti-Christian religious figures. It ends by calling for a new, revolutionary socialism based on magic, that is, on "the art of communicating with the spiritual powers in nature and in ourselves."[8] You can take this as one reminder—there are many—of the role that magic once played in political protest. (Levitate the Pentagon, anyone?) You can also see in it the interpretation of sexual categories as a special calling to transform the world in ways beyond ordinary calculation. The queer is not a simple political identity so much as a desirous vocation—a call to transform self and others through powers discoverable in sexual protest.

Queer spiritual genealogies can be connected to larger narratives of American religious inventiveness. Many movements have attracted queer adherents; each has contributed to queer reconfigurations of spiritual seeking. I leave the tangled lineages and fluid terminologies of queer authors just as I find them. My hope is that a very small selection of texts will show that queer turns to spirit or spirituality are held together by a recurring dream about what lies beyond the boundary of the ordinary—in bodies, language, or mortal desires.

Thompson: A Gallery of Gay Souls

In 1994, Mark Thompson published *Gay Soul*, interviews with "sixteen writers, healers, teachers, and visionaries." He had already edited *Gay Spirit*, a looser anthology on gay sensibility, culture, and mythmaking. "Spirit" in that title has mainly a cultural sense: community spirit, group spirit. *Gay Soul* is more selective about the authors it includes and the topics it emphasizes—not least because Thompson conducts the interviews and sets the questions. His assumptions, antipathies, and wounds stand out. The reader keeps encountering Jungian archetypes, the (alleged) failures of "social construction" and Foucault (neither of which Thompson quite understands), and the ravages of AIDS (then inescapable).

Many objections can be raised against Thompson's choice of figures in *Gay Soul*. They are all "cis-gendered" men, overwhelmingly "White," mostly middle-aged (in some broad sense), and so on. I take the interviews only as records of specific conversations. If you insist on more sweeping conclusions, Thompson's selection of established writers can remind you that there was a library of gay writing on spirituality that pushed against the furious pursuit of movement politics. Most of the writers included had been activists of one sort or another—and not just on religious issues. The interviews show that they had moved (progressed?) to other concerns. *Gay Soul* is a detailed argument that politics alone cannot sustain queer lives. If "spirituality" means many things in Thompson's book, it almost always contradicts the peremptory demands of some movement.

In most of the interviews, Thompson presses for definitions of "spirit" and "soul." There is, of course, no unanimity among the respondents. (Queer language-making is not about legislating definitions.) A few of his conversation partners resist the question or recast it before answering. For others, "soul" or "spirit" is another way of talking about God. Soul is "what we used to call God," Andrew Ramer claims (75). Clyde Hall says something similar about spirit: "People personify [spirit] as God. . . . But that's only just one manifestation of it" (128). Others contrast soul with spirit. For Harry Hay, spirit is the richer, the deeper term: It is "the distillation arising from the rich and bubbly brew in the pot, out of which new possibilities keep emerging. The world of spirit is made up of an ever-expanding continuum" (94). Hay dismisses soul as an impoverishing abstraction for religious purposes. Robert Hopcke accepts something like Hay's distinction but reverses the valuation: "When you say 'spiritual,' you think of transcending the material world. Soul is gaining that kind of knowledge without transcending" (217–18). Other conversation partners retreat from anything mystical or ritual to explain that spirituality has to do with "the relationship of the individual to the whole universe" (142, 138). Joseph Kramer reframes Thompson's question about soul and spirit with three questions of his own: "Spirituality for me is the basic question, What is life?

What is the meaning of death? And that can boil down to, Why do I breathe?" (177).

If Thompson's respondents do not agree on definitions, they do converge on aspects of being queer that were typically excluded by later programs for LGBTQ politics. I pick out three points of tacit agreement: the need for inner reform rather than outward effort; the special vocation of the gay or queer; and the danger of fixed identity, not least with regard to gender.

Thompson sometimes ends the interviews by asking what advice his conversation partner would give to a young man (*sic*) just coming out as gay. Many of the replies pivot from politics toward spiritual practice. Ram Dass imagines telling the young gay man: "Please discover who you are as quickly and directly as possible, and don't get trapped in any of the illusions your gay culture or the culture around you will try to project on you" (63). Robert Hopcke offers a similar lesson: "Your sexuality is sacred. The majority of gay men I have met see their sexuality in literal or materialistic terms and not in symbolic and sacred terms" (227). Mitch Walker is most emphatic: "For true initiation in gay spirit, the way to reach the stars is by going within. . . . That's where the real inspiration in being gay resides: It's the most direct way of knowing God" (263).

The sharpest judgment may come from Harry Hay himself—and not in response to any prompt from Thompson. Hay says, "The development of the Radical Faerie identity is probably the most advanced form of the gay movement up to the present time" (83–84). This from the one-time Marxist and founder of the Mattachine Society—the great activist. The Radical Faeries are the "most advanced form of the gay movement" because they exchange the ordinary politics of assimilation for a playful spirituality of rejection. The practice of ritual is the "most advanced" form of political activity because it can transform participants into future selves.

The emphasis on inner work over outer, on spirituality as opposed to the usual politics, is carried forward into the second tacit agreement among those Thompson interviews: the special vocation of queer folk. Sometimes the vocation is described as spiritual leadership (57–58, 122, 251). For other speakers, the task is more specific and urgent. Andrew Ramer speaks of gay men as "Midwives for the Dying" and as shamans—a view shared by many others in the volume (69–70). Hay calls up a (Socratic) image of the midwife for spiritual children, but he also argues that gay men have a special task to perform in balancing the sexes by easing the conflict of male and female (95–96; Plato, *Theaetetus* 149a–150d). The claims are not only deductions or prescriptions. *Gay Soul* appeals to visions, beginning with James Broughton's delightful story of a childhood visit from his angel (11). Here, as in Anzaldúa, there is no shame in speaking about spiritual guidance or magical sensibilities—especially as proofs of an unusual vocation.

Thompson's conversation partners repeatedly link special vocation or magical ability to androgyny. The term itself appears page after page. Those who worry about its connotations still reject a gender binary. Saslow goes furthest: "If there are five billion people on the planet, that's five billion genders" (139). The rejection of a male/female dichotomy expands to include all the other identities that depend on it. That includes "gay." ("Homosexuality" collaborates with "heterosexuality" to define desire by sex or gender.) In the middle of a critique of fixed identity, Ram Dass says, "I don't think souls themselves have any sexual identity at all" (163).

A turn inward (away from movement politics), the claim of a special vocation, the appeal to androgyny against identities: These three, at least, are shared by most of the speakers in *Gay Soul*. If movements cannot contain queerness, neither can orgasm conceived only as a physical release. Joseph Kramer, who speaks most explicitly about sexual practice as a means of enlightenment, describes himself not as a sex therapist but as "a body-based sex magician" or "a magician creating a world that doesn't exist" (175, 179). Sexual desire can be magically directed into a ceaseless pursuit of self—freed from identities, beyond the control of earthly powers, dissolved perhaps in divinity or released into Itself.

Nelson: Transitions or Mortal Tales

Maggie Nelson's *The Argonauts* begins with a question about desire. The answer is an act: *"What's your pleasure? You asked, then stuck around for an answer."*[9] The question-and-enacted-answer is part of a dispute about language. This is one of Nelson's signature devices in *The Argonauts*, the quick cut from sex to philosophy or art theory. The dispute about language starts as a contrast between two phrases. The first is HARD TO GET, which is what Nelson's friend recommends she tattoo across her knuckles. The second, in the same paragraph, is the "incantation," the magic spell, of *I love you*, which tumbles out the first time that "you" (who bears so far no other name) has anal intercourse with the narrator.[10]

The opposition between the proposed tattoo "Hard to get" and the blurted magic spell "I love you" launches a larger dispute. Quoting Wittgenstein, Nelson claims that "the inexpressible is contained—inexpressibly—in the expressed" (3). On the other hand, *"you* [still not named] had spent a lifetime equally devoted to the conviction that words are not good enough. Not only not good enough, but corrosive to all that is good, all that is real, all that is flow" (4). Nelson reads Wittgenstein while "you" keeps at bedside Samuel Beckett's *Molloy*.

A third author supplies Nelson's title: Roland Barthes, Michel Foucault's sometime lover and longtime friend. For Barthes, saying *I love you* is like "the Argonaut renewing his ship during its voyage without changing [the ship's] name . . . the very task of love and of language is to give to one and the same phrase inflections which will be forever new" (5). The irremediable ambiguity of the "you" in love talk: Gay dancers on a club floor mouth the lyrics that a diva sings to her male lover. Love songs are made for gender-shifting. Lovers reusing language rebuild a ship while sailing on it. "The very task of love and of language" (one task between them) is to give a worn-out, contaminated, commercialized phrase "inflections that will be forever new." So, too, our lovers' names: The name can stay while the person is rebuilt—or undone.

Finally, the reader learns that "you" in these pages is also named "Harry." Beyond that, things get complicated. Indeed, apart from "you," Harry's pronouns are not so clear (7). Harry likes different pronouns to mark different contexts. A character played by Harry in a movie says, "I'm a special—a two for one" (14). Reflecting on the ways that language does not fit Harry, Nelson writes:

> The answer isn't just to introduce new words (*boi, cis-gendered, andro-fag*) and then set out to reify their meanings (though obviously there is power and pragmatism here). One must also become alert to the multitude of possible uses, possible contexts, the wings with which each word can fly. Like when you whisper, *You're just a hole, letting me fill you up.* Like when I say *husband.* (8)

The last two lines could be quoted from a misogynist scene of degradation or wifely submission. They can also be—here are—a sex scene in which words fly from their ordinary uses to someplace else. In *The Argonauts*, "you" begins as an address to Harry—as the first name that Harry is given. Later, that pronoun becomes Winnicott's mother called by her infant, Nelson's baby Iggy, and Nelson herself when Harry argues with her. The inexpressible hovers around uncanny uses of the expressible.

The other side of the dispute about language, Harry's side, still remains: the subordination of language to image, presentation, or silence. Harry Dodge may still be best known as a filmmaker. The first work mentioned is the film *By Hook or by Crook* (2002). Harry also makes sculpture, does performance pieces, writes—not least, and recently, a countermemoir to *The Argonauts*.[11] Other visual and performance artists appear in *Nelson's book*, including Catherine Opie and A. L. Steiner. Nelson writes about them not as Harry's troupe but as her own figures of inspiration. This text-ship travels toward a reconciliation—a marriage, a birth-giving—of the two sides of the dispute announced by its beginning.

Perhaps unexpectedly, spirit puts in an appearance. Or it is only to be expected, since God is named right on the first page: "In this way you can have your empty church with a dirt floor swept clean of dirt and your spectacular stained glass gleaming by the cathedral rafters, both. Because nothing you can say can fuck up the place for God" (3). Nothing you can say—whether in dogmatic pronouncements, moral condemnations, or angry rejections of all religion. Pages later, Nelson appears to retract the notion of God's place: "[Anne] Carson gave a lecture . . . at which she introduced (to me) the concept of leaving space empty so that God could rush in. . . . [Now] I stare at the brackets in the Carson interview and try to enjoy them as markers of that evening from so long ago. But some revelations do not stand" (49). It is worth puzzling over those final words: "some revelations do not stand." Some revelations need to move on. Some revelations cannot be treated as fixed formulas for solving problems. Some revelations fly or get rebuilt (like the *Argos*) or take flesh in unpredictable infants. Some revelations may need to be blended with others. Nelson attributes the image of the *Argos*—of a ship being rebuilt as it sails—to Roland Barthes. But Nelson's book is called not *Argos*, the ship, but *The Argonauts*, those who sail on it. In various mythological sources, the original crew members were a remarkable mix: the demigod Hercules, the god Asclepius, Atalanta (protégée of Artemis), and many more children of divinities. Nelson's book sometimes alludes to ancient myths about the voyage, but the mythic backdrop appears most artfully when she interlaces stories about families that include divinities (in several senses). A solitary incarnation—away in a manger in Bethlehem—is displaced by the familial relations among gods and demigods and cousins of gods.

On one side: a revelation that cannot stand about leaving empty space for God. On the other side: a shipload of figures with semidivine genealogies who set off on a quest, rebuilding their means of travel as they go. These two views need not be contraries. Nelson's genre encourages juxtapositions to stand without resolution. She continues to provide emptiness in which divinities appear to make unexpected connections or transformations.

At the center of the book, Nelson presents "the many-gendered mothers of my heart" (an echo of Dana Ward). In one enumeration, the mothers include at least James Schuyler, Allen Ginsberg, Lucille Clifton, and Eve Sedgwick (105). Nelson engages Schuyler, Ginsberg, and Sedgwick at some length. She quotes Clifton only once in *The Argonauts*, though at a crucial moment (53). The many-gendered mothers supply Nelson with words for unruly bodies—queer, Black, maternal, fat. To sail with these bodies (in language and picture) until you see how flesh itself—mortal flesh, not advertising-flesh—is a full space set aside for God. If "nothing you can say can fuck up [that] place for God," some things you can say or sing or picture or perform make flesh more recognizable as divine-place.

Nelson: Language, Spirit

The Argonauts gestures repeatedly to Dodie Bellamy, who, with Judy Grahn, was counted an advocate of the "new narrative." Here are some of its techniques, listed in a retrospective essay by Robert Glück.

> We were thinking about autobiography; by autobiography we meant daydreams, nightdreams, the act of writing, the relationship to the reader, the meeting of flesh and culture, the self as collaboration, the self as disintegration, the gaps, inconsistencies and distortions, the enjambments of power, family, history and language.

In writing about sex, desire, and the body, New Narrative approached performance art, where self is put at risk by naming names, becoming naked, making the irreversible happen—the book is lived into social practice. The theme of obsessive romance did double duty, destabilizing the self and asserting gay experience.[12]

Nelson's form has strong links with New Narrative writers. It also resembles Anzaldúa's texts—or, to arrange the genealogies more exactly, *Borderlands* also registers the influence of New Narrative. But Glück's description of the shared project emphasizes effects on the reader like those described

by many of the writers in Thompson's *Gay Soul*. We find
ourselves in a thicket of references and cross-references.
Each formal experiment in the network undoes stable definitions of the gay, lesbian, trans, or queer—in Nelson most
of all. *The Argonauts* tells a poignant story about Christina
Crosby, Nelson's college teacher of feminist theory. Years
after Nelson's graduation, Crosby is invited to an undergraduate party where she is handed a card, told to write her
identity on it, and then wear it for the evening (58–59).
Nelson asks, on another page, "What sense does it make to
align 'queer' with 'sexual deviance,' when the ostensibly
straight world is having no trouble keeping pace?" (110).[13] Or
when we hand out nametags—though I keep hoping that
the undergraduate hosts were dedicated ironists.

Efforts to undo identities culminate with *The Argonauts'*
end. Nelson begins by quoting from Phillips and Bersani:
*"the joke of evolution is that it is a teleology without a point,
that we, like all animals, are a project that issues in nothing"*
(143).[14] Nelson adds—in the book's last lines: "But is there
really such a thing as nothing, as nothingness? I don't
know. I know that we're still here, who knows for how long,
ablaze with our care, its ongoing song" (143). If I can take
"care" as a form of desire and song as one refinement of
speech, then Nelson ends by exhorting readers to stretch
desire through bodies by pulling language. The space of
the unknown future is the place for divinities best invoked
by writing out song.

The queer is not the performance of acts in certain genital configurations. It is a torque of the gender binary, that
foundation for so many social hierarchies. Nelson offers
unabashed sexual descriptions as a "cis-gendered woman" of
unannounced "sexual orientation" who is in an intensely
erotic relationship with someone in transition. Queerness
remains transgression, but the transgression is not only or

mainly in genital pairings, sexual acrobatics, or dexterity with "toys." The transgression occurs in the firm hope that some erotic excess points to an unexhausted capacity for human transformation—for our songs. The excess cannot be contained by marriage, partnership, reproduction, or allegorical readings of the *Song of Songs*. I also emphasize: It cannot be captured by any literal taxonomy, no matter how pious.

Another New Narrative

Once upon a time, when I was twenty, I spent a year trying to write my days. In their least events, I hoped to glimpse the face of God.

I did not think myself particularly holy. Quite the opposite: I was squeezed hard by my failure to live what I had promised during my recent baptism. Still, I believed that if I looked intently enough—wrote acutely enough—I would see a little divinity.

Was I seeking ecstatic rapture? A dream-vision orchestrated for angelic choirs? Did I long to be transported to the end of history as witness of the grand apocalypse? No. If I expected anything, it was some translucence, a glimpse of the first light that carried the whole creation as a hint. But it would be more candid to say that I did not know what I wanted to find unless it was the motive for my wanting. It was like knowing that the love of your life awaits you impatiently—only you can't find either an address or a recent photo.

That year, I received a traveling fellowship to visit Christian monasteries in Europe. My fantasy of an itinerary was scrambled almost at once, by forces external and internal. So, I decided to spend months in Ireland and then in Mexico, looking in on contemplative communities, making pilgrimages to religious sites, but mostly writing. For hours each day. Sometimes in a sort of ecstasy, automatically. At other times, in obedience to almost paralyzing deliberation. I wrote lament and unkind self-exposure and descriptions void of life. On the best days, I tried to transcribe sequences of thoughts or feelings in their flow. Every few weeks, I would go back over the scribbles to add pieces of the daily Roman Catholic liturgy then in use—the appointed Eucharistic texts and pieces of daily prayers, "the hours." The additions were supposed to strike sparks from the recorded events.

But they were not events in any ordinary sense. There were long hours of silence in days spent mostly alone. I did not read much beyond the Christian Bible and prayer books. I had a little music on a cassette player for moments when homesickness or loneliness turned harsh. Mostly I waited for something to show or show up.

I walked a lot. In Ireland: from Cappoquin, where I had a room, to Mount Melleray, a Trappist abbey. Grey Gothic rising from an asphalt parking lot. A balcony for visitors looking down on the long church. I took other walks that year near an empty Jesuit novitiate in Louisiana, where I went on retreat. Then roads in Mexico, some of them familiar from my childhood.

Once, after long prayer, the world shimmered with golden light. Months later, the ghosts of a ruined Dominican house clustered around me like the red-orange blossoms blowing from a tree called Flamboyant, *flamboyán*. Near the year's end, on a sidewalk in a lakeside village, a sudden splash of sun on my face through palm fronds brought half a minute of complete tranquility.

During my year of wandering, I tried to live a monastic celibacy. I do not remember kissing anyone. Certainly there was no genital sex with another body. In the Irish city of Cork, the manager of the guesthouse urged me to go out dancing.

The possibility had never occurred to me. I did spend one Friday night watching across the Lee River as traffic headed into the city. How many were going on dates? It was like speculating about life on distant planets.

In March or April, I was renting a small house on Lake Chapala in Mexico. My former teacher sent one of his current seniors down to talk with me about college. I was twenty-one, he was eighteen. Tall and angular, he moved his hands gracefully or stilled them in perfect repose.

Oh, I realized, looking at his hands. Oh.

He got back on the bus and returned to the city.

That was the whole of my epiphany.

Stories about spirit need not, after all, sound so unusual. You can go looking for God in monasteries and find your erotic desire. You can pursue your erotic desire only to encounter divinities.

Having written tens of thousands of words about my year of pilgrimage, I tried to reach down into them, to touch some ground. I remembered the old Christian practice of "negative" theology. It is sometimes presented as a preliminary rule in theological grammar, a sort of finger-wagging to be performed at the beginning of a magnum opus. At other times, it appears as a detour through that remote field known—or mocked—as mystical theology. But negative theology is neither a grammatical caution nor a fringe phenomenon. It is an event that rewrites our pretensions, especially in regard to love. It alters our relation to language. We no longer speak or write to compile facts. We inhabit language to be cast beyond it, by it.

The spiritual is in daily life or not at all. It already moves through our bodies as they are—or not at all. If "spiritual" language can sometimes rush through all the poetic devices of exhortation and ecstasy, it begins by loosening daily speech—say, in parables.

Writing about spirit need not dwell on it as a topic. It may hesitate ever to name it. Especially in a wasteland of broken religions, the divine is best spoken otherwise than by confident naming. That might be true of sex and gender as well, since they are linked to the divine and persecuted in the name of God.

How much you can speak any of this must remain uncertain.

Epilogue: The Impossibility of Being E(a)rnest

A few years ago, I began to offer an undergraduate course on sexual ethics within the college's core curriculum. Explicitly, it was guided by two questions: Why might you seek a sexual ethics? What language would you need to articulate it? Because the course had to squeeze into a curricular cubbyhole originally hammered together for philosophy, it spent some sessions on "ethical reasoning" and assigned philosophical essays. But I also insisted from the first meeting that sexual ethics in the United States could not be understood apart from dominant religious traditions and terminologies. Beneath that bland historical commonplace, a third guiding question was implied: Do you seek something through sex beyond the sociopolitical goals announced in high school sex ed (if you were lucky enough to receive any)?

Teaching the course was regularly satisfying and sometimes delightful. Most of the students gave themselves generously to the work. Their final projects were astonishingly inventive. A few of them came to tell me afterward how the course had changed their thinking or helped with private pains. More publicly, the course showed a spreading recognition of sex/gender variation. It was led by an openly "gay" man and staffed by teaching fellows diverse in many ways: their sexual or gender "identity," their race or ethnicity, their nationality or first language, and so on. The hundred and fifty students enrolled for any semester displayed notable tolerance for varieties of sexual acts and attractions. For example, the Victorian lecture hall (finished two years before Oscar Wilde visited the campus) and the scattered section rooms witnessed animated discussions of many controversial issues but not of the rightness of homosexuality. That was as much taken for granted as the need for consent or the evil of child abuse.

Teaching the course was also taxing. Most of the pedagogical challenges were familiar. Still, and from the first semester, I began to notice how often some of the students performed *knowingness*.[1] No matter how unusual or arcane the sexual taste I might mention, heads in the lecture hall would nod as if to say, "Oh, that? Of course." I gathered from office conversations and college surveys of incoming students that their sexual experience was likely to be limited. Yet, if I mentioned polyamorous mystical societies devoted to barking play in alien costumes, heads would bob. Perhaps I exaggerate—a little.

You might reply, chuckling or sighing, that this was just adolescent boasting or the reflex of students never permitted to admit ignorance on any topic. I would agree with you. But there is something more here: a societal imperative to privilege expertise about sex/gender over embodied discovery. As if there were no need to learn from experience about one's own (changing) desire(s), orientation(s), gender(s). As if the code of one's own sex/gender could best be deciphered in advance by certified cryptographers. Knowingness in the lecture hall may have been boasting or status anxiety, but it was also a microcosm of the dominant forms of speech about sex. No matter how often I pulled off the magisterial mask, I found that mimicry in myself too. Worse: I was paid to give expert lectures on sex.

Sometimes, in our discussions, knowingness would express itself as brazen (scientific, ethical) confidence: "You can know *with certainty* your own sexual orientation before having much or any sexual experience." "You can know *in advance* the requirements for your best sexual experiences." "You can correctly predict now the *future course* of your sexed/gendered selfhood." This kind of knowingness is more than boasting about your acquaintance with sexology. It is the faith in a sexology ready to be *spoken*. Knowingness is more than a claim to possess knowledge. It is the affirmation that there is a knowledge waiting to be possessed and then professed. Sex/gender can be known, and its knowledge ensures articulate application. No assembly required.

Oscar Wilde's best-known play puns in its title on the ear's confusion between a virtue or quality of character and a proper or "Christian" name: "earnest" and "Ernest." On its surface, the title commends earnestness. It is important to be earnest—not least by being truthful about one's name. Just below the surface, of course, the play causes all kinds of trouble about receiving, keeping, and exchanging names. It also suggests, to anyone listening seriously to its frivolity, that there is no way to be earnestly Ernest—if, that is, you invest that name with the fantasies shared by Gwendolen and Cecily. You cannot forecast your destiny in love on the basis of proper names. More: No proper name guarantees its bearer the happy ending of a romantic comedy.

So many queer campaigns to revolutionize speech are haunted by fantasies of correct classification. They both resent and desire names with the power to disclose an essence—or, at least, a plan for social assimilation. The campaigns discard older names because they are so eager to impose *real* ones. Alas, these mostly repackage prevailing expectations. Like the wish for symmetry: You can hear it in the resemblance between "homosexual" and "heterosexual," in the awkward naming of "bisexuality," in the demand for *same*-sex marriage, in the well-intentioned question whether you like boys or girls. It goes without saying that the liking must be the same; only its object can change. But what if the liking is different? And what, after all, does it mean to talk about the *object* of sexual desire? Is it genital anatomy? Ways to give and get pleasure? A culturally stabilized gender—specific mannerisms, styles of movement and dress, social roles? The shape of eyebrows, the tint of eyes? All of the above? Fill in the blank, but do not exceed the space provided.

The revolutionary campaigns are typically earnest. They often prescribe fundamentalist terminologies. They permit ironies or jokes only at the expense of others. But what if the only half-adequate languages for human sex/gender are not literal? What if they are spiritual—that is, preparatory, poetic, visionary? What if they *must* be camp?

Despite progress in decriminalization, toleration, and assimilation, one important promise of movements for sexual freedom has not been fulfilled. We were all promised—"queer" and "straight" alike—better ways for living transformed sex. We are still waiting.

There are many reasons why this revolutionary promise has not been kept—and why it could not be. Some of them arise from the choice of terms. A category like "sexual identity" implies fixed boundaries around human erotic development, which prescribe in turn efficient means of intervention, which rest in their turn on a carefully delimited picture of human fulfillment. The category implies a character. The model, the means, and the assumptions together forestall any need in the character for a robust ethics. Indeed, they constitute an antiethics so far as they imply the fixity of a transparent self whose causes and boundaries can be known in advance. If "revolution" means a sociopolitical movement, then a revolution cannot supply an adequate sex/gender ethics because our sex/gender is not wholly a sociopolitical project. Even if it were, an effort to revolutionize it would have to suppose that human groups control the most important sociopolitical forces, know just when to apply them, and can apply them consistently for the good.

Keeping the promise to speak queer ethics requires richer queer languages. As many of this book's writers have shown, that is not so simple as changing a few terms or unfurling a permanent blueprint for self-labeling. To change language, you have to change the way human beings use language. That includes shifting their picture of how words can mean. Walcott, again: "To change your language you must change your life." Changing your life will include learning language otherwise.

When I teach ethics, I start (as Socrates did) with language. I propose that we cultivate a multilingualism deeply suspicious of the literal, eager to undo tacit coercions, and rich in incitements to ethical improvisation. This improvisation will begin by refusing to assume postures of knowingness. It looks instead for schools that might be communities of transformative *askêsis*, that might offer exercises in fashioning language, that have a liturgy for remembering that there is something uncontainable in whatever constitutes a human life.

Some recent queer language has been hollowed by the silences around queer deaths. (Consider the craving for identities as a wish for some kind of survival—like a warrior's trust in the "immortality" of fame.) Deaths from assault or execution but also in plague—especially that plague once too shameful for a president to mention, much less to treat or prevent. "Silence = Death." Those two words, linked by the equal sign, recapitulate centuries of our condition and our punitive end, because a sodomite burned at the stake received only the foretaste of a punitive eternity. I know that the design, made famous by ACT UP, inverts the Nazi triangle, that the equation is an urgent call to action: "Never Again!" I know that, but I continue to regard queer language as a ceaseless call without guaranteed response, vulnerable to violence or amnesia; a tender plant, liable to wither under untimely frosts but sometimes able to produce seed; a mortal body that may return to the common languages more than what it received.

There is no point in pretending to have eternal essences, to win final battles, to lead irreversible revolutions. Nor can we gather a team to complete the great cosmic encyclopedia of queerness that will comprise all "our" past, present, and future. Whatever else we may be, we are speaking mortal bodies with the capacity for sex—or sexed bodies with the uncanny but transient *facultad* for speech. To paraphrase Hedwig of the Angry Inch: That's what we've got to work with.[2]

What we have to work with: candid acknowledgments of mortal incompleteness, historical persecutions, dazzling languages almost lost, personal and communal failures in courage or imagination. If we continue to speak, these become so many offerings to desire—and so many testimonies of its changeable persistence. My testimony is not that desire remains unchanged in its panting pursuit. On the contrary: It changes, it changes. Change must then be the vocation of any calling that wants to be queer.

There is another way of hearing that line in Alfred Douglas's poem: "I am the Love that dare not speak its name." What if the Love is not silenced only from outside, by lethal shame or animal muteness? What if it *dare* not speak its name because it recognizes that no ethics has yet been prepared for its manifold ways of life?

The work of queer literature—or queer thinking—is not to find new labels for the identical boxes on an endless sorting bench. Queer language-making wants ethical narratives for lives that have not yet been lived. If what lives under the label "homosexuality" is neither sin nor crime nor disease nor social problem nor revolutionary provocation nor market segment, what could it be? And where could one find language for a response to that question now?

In the last week of the course on sexual ethics, I repeat: Please *do not* imagine that my ending is a conclusion.

Acknowledgments

The invitation to write a short book about sex/gender identities came from Doug Mitchell in the summer of 2016. Having acquired some of my earlier books over two decades, he wanted one more. Within two years, he began to talk of it as our last project: A prognosis had turned grim. I could not finish writing fast enough.

After Doug's death, with changes at the publishing house, I almost abandoned the project. Susan Stinson persuaded me to keep writing toward it. She also helped me escape many of the traps of academic style. If others still hold me, the fault is mine.

During the years of rewriting, two colleagues gave me occasions for testing my thoughts before audiences. Kent Brintnall was my host for talks at the University of North Carolina in Charlotte. Peng Yin taught versions of the manuscript to seminary classes at Emory University and Boston University.

I began writing this book as a regular faculty member of Harvard's Divinity School. I finish it—force myself to stop—in retirement. I am grateful to the school for its support. I am more grateful still to the conversation partners I encountered there as students.

Notes

Prologue: Our Names, Our Destinies!

1. I follow the three-act version in Isobel Murray's *Oscar Wilde: The Major Works* (Oxford: Oxford University Press, 2000), here 490. I also keep an eye on the actor's manuscript in Harvard's Houghton Library, MS Thr 574.

2. Berthold Brecht, *Die Dreigroschenoper, nach John Gays "The Beggar's Opera"* (Berlin: Suhrkamp, 1969), 50. Unless otherwise noted, all translations are my own.

3. Behind Foucault, alongside him, there stand several hundred others who taught me about these questions. To acknowledge each of them fairly would require more than footnotes; it would mean retelling decades of learning. But that is another book, a memoir of private gratitude. This book will only cite authors when it quotes them or relies on their particular evidence.

4. Reported by Christian Gury, "Le Congrés au fil de jours," *Arcadie* 307–308 (July–August 1979): 506.

5. Foucault, *Surveiller et punir* (Paris: Gallimard, 1975), 27, emphasis added.

6. These are stage directions from Hélène Cixous's play *Portrait de Dora* (Paris: Éditions des Femmes, 1976), 23.

7. Ari Banias, *Anybody: Poems* (New York, 2016), 84–86, after Lauren Berlant, *Cruel Optimism* (Durham, NC: Duke University Press, 2011), esp. chap. 4, 121–59.

8. Eve Kosofsky Sedgwick, *Epistemology of the Closet* (Berkeley: University of California Press, 1990), 1–63.

9. Mark D. Jordan, *The Invention of Sodomy in Christian Theology* (Chicago: University of Chicago Press, 1997).

Linguistic Orientations

1. Ludwig Wittgenstein, *Philosophical Investigations*, 4th rev. ed., trans. G. E. M. Anscombe, P. M. S. Hacker, and Joachim Schulte (Chichester: Wiley-Blackwell, 2009), p. 11, sect. 18. I cite this edition parenthetically by section number as *PI*.

2. For a summary of the chief editorial problems, see *PI*, xviii–xxiii. The original editors, Anscombe and Rhees, did not aim to produce anything like a critical edition. They hoped rather to compose a readable text—that is, a text recognizable in their academic circles as creditable philosophy.

3. Norman Malcolm, "A Memoir," in his *Ludwig Wittgenstein: A Memoir, rev. ed.* (Oxford: Oxford University Press, 1984), 27.

4. Georg Henrik von Wright, "A Biographical Sketch," in Malcolm, *Ludwig Wittgenstein*, 3.

5. For a much larger collection of such remarks, see James C. Klagge, *Wittgenstein in Exile* (Cambridge, MA: MIT Press, 2011).

6. Ludwig Wittgenstein, *Remarks on Colour*, ed. G. E. M. Anscombe (Oxford: Blackwell, 1977), I.67, I.55 (pp. 11, 9), quoted in Derek Jarman, *Chroma: A Book of Colour—June '93* (1994; rpt. London: Vintage, 2000), 1. I follow Wittgenstein's German.

7. Wittgenstein, *Remarks on Colour*, I.13, p. 4.

8. Eve Kosofsky Sedgwick, *Touching Feeling: Affect, Pedagogy, Performativity* (Durham, NC: Duke University Press, 2003), 6. I cite this book parenthetically as *TF*.

9. Eve Kosofsky Sedgwick, *Epistemology of the Closet* (Berkeley: University of California Press, 1990), 22.

10. James Merrill's piece was originally published as "Japan: A Prose of Departure," *New York Review of Books* 33, no. 20 (December 18, 1986): 13–18. It was reprinted with some alterations under the shortened title that Sedgwick recalls in *The Inner Room* (New York: Knopf, 1988), 53–72.

11. Eve Kosofsky Sedgwick, *A Dialogue on Love* (Boston: Beacon, 2000). I cite this book parenthetically as *DL* Sedgwick does imitate Merrill's forms throughout. Her poems, like Merrill's in "A Prose of Departure," are mostly three-line haikus of seventeen syllables (often five-seven-five). More significantly, Sedgwick sets her therapist's case notes in small caps. She reminds the reader of Merrill's Ephraim, "the small-caps speaking spirit summoned through a Ouija board" (137).

1. A Quarrel of Queer Glossaries

1. Samuel Johnson, *A Dictionary of the English Language . . .* (London: W. Strahan and others, 1755), entry for "Glossary."

2. *Regina v. Wilde* (April 26–May 1, 1895). The report of the various trials in the records of the Central Criminal Court sessions, vols. 121–22 (April–June 1895) contains none of the evidence.

3. H. Montgomery Hyde, *Trials of Oscar Wilde* (London: W. Hodge, [1948]), 236. A slightly different version of the speech is given in *The Trial of Oscar Wilde from the Shorthand Reports* (Paris: [privately printed], 1906), 58–59.

4. Alfred Douglas, "Two Loves," *The Chameleon* [London] 1, no. 1 (December 1894): 26–28.

5. For a sampling of Linnaean puns and scandalized reactions to them, see Andrea Wulf, *The Brother Gardeners: Botany, Empire, and the Birth of an Obsession* (New York: Vintage, 2010), 58–65. The history of sex/gender languages is in no small part a history of fantastic "sciences." Four decades ago, John Boswell recalled the ancient zoology that passed directly into Christian moral theology. See his *Christianity, Social Tolerance, Homosexuality* (Chicago: University of Chicago Press, 1980), esp. 137–58.

6. For a reply, see Mary Wollstonecraft's *A Vindication of the Rights of Women* (London: J. Johnson, 1791), 209.

7. H. L. Mencken, "The Blushful Mystery," in *Prejudices: First, Second, and Third Series* (New York: Library of America, 2010), 117.

8. Amy Lowell, *Pictures of a Floating World* (1919, rpt. Boston: Houghton Mifflin, 1921).

9. Mario Praz, *The Romantic Agony*, trans. Angus Davidson (Cleveland: Meridian, 1956), 31.

10. From this point forward, I shift to John Sturrock's recent translation, *Sodom and Gomorrah* (New York: Penguin, 2005), 1, which I cite as *SG*. I compare it with the French text in Proust, *À la recherche du temps perdu*, ed. Jean-Yves Tadié, vol. 3, Bibliothèque de la Pléiade (Paris: NRF/Gallimard, 1988).

11. As I sort interlaced vocabularies, I move back and forth across the text. It would be impractical to cite all the instances mentioned. The reader who feels compelled to check my work is invited to reread *SG*, 1–33. Many other passages in Proust's series treat homoerotic topics. They have been studied by such expert readers as Eve Kosofsky Sedgwick and Didier Eribon.

12. By one reckoning of the novel's chronology, it is the spring of 1900. The Narrator is twenty-two or twenty-three. See Jacques Darriulat, "Marcel Proust, A la recherche du temps perdu: Propositions pour une chronologie," http://www.jdarriulat .net/Auteurs/Proust/ChronoProust.html.

13. Carl Westphal, "Die conträre Sexualempfindung, Symptom eines neuropathischen (psychopathischen) Zustandes," *Archiv für Psychiatrie und Nervenkrankheiten* 2, no. 1 (1869): 73–108, esp. 107n. See Michel Foucault, *Histoire de la sexualité*, vol. 1: *La volonté de savoir* (Paris: NRF/Gallimard, 1976), 59.

14. French dictionaries give a published example from 1899. The *Oxford English Dictionary* lists English uses from private correspondence in 1892. Such dates are, at best, rough indications of early use.

15. Note the Narrator's objection to the term "homosexuality" when he first mentions it: "what is sometimes quite wrongly called homosexuality" (*SG*, 9). He does not explain the error.

16. Note that *identité* means here sameness. The next chapter will show through other examples how easily the sameness of shared characteristics becomes—especially in combination with race or ethnicity—an identity that constitutes individuals.

17. The original edition is Richard Meeker [Forman Brown], *Better Angel* (New York: Greenberg, 1933). I cite (as *BA*) the more accessible version with a revised introduction by Hubert Kennedy and an epilogue by Brown in his own name (3rd ed.; Boston: Alyson, 1995). The novel was also reissued in pulp format under the title *Torment* (New York: Universal Publishing, 1951).

18. Meeker, *BA*, 132 ("homosexual," "highly scientific"), 170 ("invert"), 79 ("queer," in quotation marks), 80 ("scum," "decadent perverts"), 176 ("'perversion'—how he loathed the word"), 190 ("fairies," in quotation marks), 195 ("pansies").

19. In the King James Version, "spiritual" appears frequently in Pauline texts as a translation for *pneumatikos* (e.g., 1 Cor. 2:13,15; 3:1; 9:11; 10:3–4; 12:1; 14:1,12,37; 15:15:44,46).

20. Graham Greene, "Fiction Chronicle," *The Tablet*, November 14, 1936, 678b, emphasis added.

21. Philip Herring, *Djuna: The Life and Work of Djuna Barnes* (New York: Viking, 1995), 254.

22. Djuna Barnes, *Nightwood* (New York: New Directions, 2006), 87.

23. Jerome, *Liber interpretationis hebraicorum nominum*, De Genesi "S," ed. Paul de Lagarde (Turhout: Brepols, 1959), 71, ll. 18–19.

2. Inventions of Identity

1. For a concise general account, see Philip Gleason, "Identifying Identity: A Semantic History," *Journal of American History* 6, no. 4 (March 1983): 910–31, as revised for his *Speaking of Diversity* (Baltimore, MD: Johns Hopkins University Press, 1992), 123–49. My story disagrees with narratives about the discovery of "sexual identity" in the current sense at or before the beginning of the twentieth century. See, for one recent example, Robert Beachy,

Gay Berlin: Birthplace of a Modern Identity (New York: Vintage, 2015), beginning with x–xvii.

2. Erik H. Erikson, *Childhood and Society* (New York: Norton, 1950), 281. I cite this first edition parenthetically as *CS*. In the early 1960s, Erikson revised the book for a second edition.

3. Sigmund Freud, "Address to the Society of B'nai B'rith," in the *Standard Edition of the Complete Psychological Works of Sigmund Freud*, ed. James Strachey (London: Hogarth, 1959), 20:273. The German text Erikson reads is "Ansprach an die Mitglieder des Vereins B'nai B'rith," in *Gesammelte Werke: chronologisch geordnet* (London: Imago, 1941), 17:49–53.

4. Erik Erikson, "The Problem of Ego Identity," *Journal of the American Psychoanalytic Association* 4 (1956): 57, emphasis added.

5. I paraphrase Michel Foucault, "Nietzsche, la généalogie, l'histoire," in *Hommage à Jean Hippolite* (Paris: Presses universitaires de France, 1971), 145–72.

6. Thomas Colley, "The Nature and Origins of Psychological Sexual Identity," *Psychological Review* 66, no. 3 (1959): 165–77. I will refer to this paper parenthetically as *NO*.

7. John William Money, "Hermaphroditism: An Inquiry into the Nature of a Human Paradox," PhD diss., Harvard University, 1952, part I, 2. I cite this dissertation using section and page numbers.

8. The current edition of the *Oxford English Dictionary* judges that the use of "gender" to name sociocultural expressions is a US coinage but points to its appearance a decade before Money finished the dissertation. It cites as its first example Madison Bentley, "Safety and Hazard in Childhood," *American Journal of Psychology* 58 (1945): 228. The word "role" is applied to cultural expectations of femininity and masculinity throughout Margaret Mead's *Male and Female* (published 1949, after being delivered as public lectures in 1946). "Role" also appears in Erikson's *Childhood and Society* (1950), often as a synonym for "identity."

9. John Money, Joan Hampson, and John Hampson, "An Examination of Some Basic Sexual Concepts: The Evidence of Human Hermaphroditism," *Bulletin of Johns Hopkins Hospital*

97, no. 4 (October 1955): 302n. See esp. 310, where establishing a gender is likened to settling into "a native language."

10. For example, John Money, *The Psychologic Study of Man* (Springfield, IL: Charles C. Thomas, 1957), 51.

11. For example, Edward Thomas Devine and Paul Underwood Kellogg, *The Survey* 52 [New York: Survey Associates] (1924): iv, 122, 234, 262, 601, 609.

12. For example, Donald Webster Cory (pseud.), *The Homosexual in America: A Subjective Approach* (Castle Books, 1960), 81, 181, 209; Irving Bieber et al., *Homosexuality: A Psychoanalytic Study of Male Homosexuals* (New York: Basic Books, 1962), 12, 14.

13. Erving Goffman, *Stigma: Notes on the Management of Spoiled Identity* (Englewood Cliffs, NJ: Prentice-Hall, 1963), 57 (emphasis added), 4.

14. For example, John Money, "Factors in the Genesis of Homosexuality," in *Determinants of Human Sexual Behavior*, ed. G. Winokur (Springfield, IL: C. C. Thomas, 1963), 19–43.

15. For example, Robert Stoller, "The Hermaphroditic Identity of Hermaphrodites," *Journal of Nervous and Mental Disease* 137/1 (1964): 453–457, at 453.

16. Thomas Buckley, "A Changing of Sex by Surgery Began at Johns Hopkins," *New York Times*, November 21, 1966.

17. I use the collated text at https://queerrhetoric.wordpress.com/2011/04/03/the-woman-identified-woman/#note.

18. Stoller, "The Hermaphroditic Identity of Hermaphrodites," 453, 457.

19. Goffman, *Stigma*, throughout, but more specifically Franklin E. Kameny, "Gay Is Good," in *The Same Sex: An Appraisal of Homosexuality*, ed. Ralph W. Weltge (Philadelphia: Pilgrim, 1969), 141. Compare James Colton, "The Homosexual Identity," *Ladder* 12, nos. 11–12 (1968): 8.

20. William Shakespeare, *The Tempest*, 5.1.

21. For example, Allen Young, "On Human and Gay Identity: A Liberationist Dilemma," *Fag Rag / Gay Sunshine*, Stonewall 5th Anniversary Issue (Summer 1974): 31–32.

22. For example, Joel D. Hencken and William T. O'Dowd, "Coming Out as an Aspect of Identity Formation," *Gai saber* 1, no. 1 (Spring 1977): 18–22.

23. Even to list the available overviews of older debates is daunting. I might start with *Radical History Review* 20 (1979), *Salmagundi* 58–59 (1982–1983), and Edward Stein's *Forms of Desire* (1992).

24. An eloquent, elusive instance is Leo Bersani's *Homos* (Cambridge, MA: Harvard University Press, 1995). See, for example, the critique of "immobilizing definitions of identity" (76).

25. Joseph Epstein, "Homo/Hetero: The Struggle for Sexual Identity," *Harper's Magazine*, September 1970, 37–51.

26. I follow the eyewitness account in Arthur Bell, *Dancing the Gay Lib Blues: A Year in the Homosexual Liberation Movement* (New York: Simon and Schuster, 1971), 131–35.

27. Unsigned article, "After Hours: Little Boy Brummel," *Harper's Magazine*, September 1, 1954, 94: "but since *Mademoiselle* advertises 'India pants' for both sexes it can't be for lack of opportunity. In short, a time of turmoil and indeterminate sexual identity."

28. Merle Miller, "What It Means to Be Homosexual," *New York Times Magazine*, January 17, 1971, 57, 60.

29. See, for example, *State of N.J. v. Henry A. Vigiliano* (decided July 7, 1964), 202 A.2d 657, at 665; *United States v. Robert F. Norton* (decided May 19, 1972), 45 C.M.R. 642; *In the matter of the tenure hearing of Paula M. Grossman* (decided February 20, 1974), 316 A.2d 39; and so on.

30. To mention only two obvious examples: M. V. Lee Badgett, "The Wage Effects of Sexual Orientation Discrimination," *ILR Review* 48, no. 4 (July 1995): 726–39; William N. Eskridge Jr. and Nan D. Hunter, *Sexuality, Gender, and the Law* (Westbury, NY: Foundation Press, 1997).

Interlude with Exercises: How ~~We~~ Talk ~~Now~~

1. Samuel Johnson, *A Dictionary of the English* Language, preface, [v]. I cite this folio edition parenthetically as *D*, assigning page numbers as we now count them.

2. Harvard University, Office of Diversity, Inclusion, and Belonging, *Foundational Concepts and Affirming Language* (2020), 9, emphasis added. The next quotation also comes from this page.

3. Office of Diversity and Inclusion, Amherst College, *Common Language Guide* (2019).

4. See, for example, Gore Vidal, "Sex Is Politics," *Playboy*, January 1979, reprinted in *Gore Vidal: Sexually Speaking, Collected Sex Writings*, ed. Donald Weise (San Francisco: Cleis, 1999), 110.

5. For this conflation of identifying *with* and identifying *as*, see Eve Kosofsky Sedgwick, *Epistemology of the Closet* (Berkeley: University of California Press, 1990), 61–62.

6. In *Advocate* classifieds at the end of 1991, there are twenty-six symbols (excluding credit card logos). They include a variety of sexual tastes. They do not include race or ethnicity.

7. "List of Sexualities," Sexuality Wiki, https://sexuality.fandom.com/wiki/List_of_Sexualities.

8. "Gender Identities," Gender Wiki, https://gender.fandom.com/Category:Gender_Identities.

9. David Halperin offers a trenchant description of the inadequacy of gay identity as an expression of gay subjectivity: *How to Be Gay (Cambridge, MA: Harvard University Press, 2012)*, 69–76. I agree emphatically but remain stubbornly curious about how our ordinary language makes sexual identities sound dependable.

10. Michelle Cliff, *Claiming an Identity They Taught Me to Despise* (Watertown, MA: Persephone, 1980).

11. Susan Sontag, "Notes on Camp," *Partisan Review* 31 (1964): 515. This version contains errors of fact in the examples that were corrected before Sontag reprinted the essay in *Against Interpretation* (1966).

3. Identities at Prayer

1. To offer just one satirical example, "Report of a Meeting of the Amateur Celibacy Society, Junior Branch," *Punch* 46 (April 6, 1864): 162–63, which smacks its lips over vestments.

2. Evelyn Waugh, *Brideshead Revisited* (Boston: Little, Brown, 1945), 22.

3. Havelock Ellis and John Addington Symonds, *Studies in the Psychology of Sex*, vol. 1, *Sexual Inversion* (London: Wilson and MacMillan, 1897). I cite the text parenthetically as *SI*. The monograph's textual history is complicated. For an expert summary, see the critical edition by Ivan Crozier (New York: Palgrave Macmillan, 2008), 1–95.

4. I follow *SI*, 165. The original edition is John Addington Symonds, *A Problem in Greek Ethics, Being an Inquiry into the Phenomenon of Sexual Inversion, Addressed Especially to Medical Psychologists and Jurists* (London: Privately printed for the APEOPAGITIGA [*sic*] Society, 1908), 1.

5. [Edward Carpenter], *Homogenic Love* (Manchester: Labour, 1894).

6. I speak here of "sexual identity," not identity generally. The basic notion of identity crossed earlier into Christian self-description. See, for a popular example, Will Herberg, *Protestant, Catholic, Jew: An Essay in American Religious Sociology* (Chicago: University of Chicago Press, 1955), 11–13, 16, 31, 40, and so on.

7. It was shepherded to press by Bailey under the title, *Sexual Offenders and Social Punishment* (Westminster: Church Information Board, 1956).

8. See the report by Donald S. Lucas, *The Homosexual and the Church* (San Francisco: Mattachine Society, 1966).

9. For example, W. Norman Pittenger, *Time for Consent: A Christian's Approach to Homosexuality* (London: SCM, 1967), 11, denying any "identity" between male and female homosexuals. There is no change in this terminology for the revised third edition (1976); see the examples on 20, 32, 58.

10. W. Dwight Oberholtzer, *Is Gay Good?* (Philadelphia: Westminster, 1971), 61n43 (citing Lofland), 282n237 (citing Hooker).

11. All three quotations come from the italicized headnote to Nicholas Benton, *God and My Gay Soul* (Berkeley: Committee of Concern for Homosexuals, [1971]), 1.

12. Ginny Benson, "Reformism: The Politics of Ostriches," *Motive* 32, no. 1 (1972): 48. Compare Charlotte Bunch and Rita

Mae Brown, "What Every Lesbian Should Know," *Motive* 32, no. 1 (1972): 4.

13. Roy Eddey and Michael Ferri, "Editorial: Approaching Lavender," *Motive* 32, no. 2 (1972), 2–3.

14. John Preston, "Beyond Rhetoric," *Motive* 32, no. 2 (1972): 14, emphasis added. Along with many others, Preston capitalizes "Gay" as if it were a proper name. A year earlier, Preston had published "Gay, Proud and Christian," *Event: Issues and Viewpoints for Laymen* 11, no. 3 (March 1971): 17–20. He writes there of a "Gay identity" as an "expression of sexual identity" but also of "a Gay subculture," "the Gay world," "the Gay life style," and (in the phrase favored by early members of the Mattachine Society) "our people."

15. John W. Gill, "The Gay Identity Movement," in *Theology and Body*, ed. John Y. Fenton (Philadelphia: Westminster, 1974), 86, 88–89.

16. Ralph Blair, *An Evangelical Looks at Homosexuality* (New York: Homosexual Community Counseling Center, 1977), 10. The text was originally published in 1972 under the title "The Gay Evangelical," in *Homosexuality and Religion*, Otherwise Monograph series no. 13 (National Task Force on Student Personnel Services and Homosexuality, 1972). I quote the 1977 pamphlet version.

17. Ralph Blair, "Student Personnel Perspectives and Homosexually Interested College Students," EdD diss., Pennsylvania State University, 1971.

18. William R. Johnson, "The Good News of Gay Liberation," in Sally Gearhart and Johnson, *Loving Women/Loving Men: Gay Liberation and the Church* (San Francisco: Glide, 1974), 94. I cite the book parenthetically as *LW*.

19. Compare Robert Treese, "Homosexuality: A Contemporary View of the Biblical Perspective," for the Consultation on Theology and the Homosexual, August 22–24, 1966. The phrase "the theological issue of homosexuality" (1966) becomes "a theological stance on the issue of homosexual identity" (1973).

20. For example, Ralph W. Weltge, "The Paradox of Man and Woman," in *The Same Sex: An Appraisal of Homosexuality*, ed. Ralph W. Weltge (Philadelphia: Pilgrim, 1969), 63: "The name

homosexual is a mythical identity . . . a metonym for a real man whose identity transcends his sex history."

21. John J. McNeill, *The Church and the Homosexual* (Kansas City, MO: Sheed, Andrews, & McMeel, 1976), 106–7.

22. J. Gordon Melton, ed., *The Churches Speak on: Homosexuality* (Detroit: Gale Research, 1991), 113–15.

23. I follow the text in Melton, *The Churches Speak on: Homosexuality*, 147 (emphasis and numeration added).

24. Anita Bryant, *The Anita Bryant Story* (Old Tappan, NJ: Revell, 1977), 55. Her source is George F. Gilder, *Sexual Suicide* (New York: Bantam, 1974). Gilder speaks of "sexual identity" throughout as an expression of the fundamental dichotomy between male and female (e.g., 18).

25. Elizabeth R. Moberly, *Psychogenesis, the Early Development of Gender Identity* (London: Routledge and Kegan Paul, 1983), esp. chap. 3.

26. Elizabeth R. Moberly, *Homosexuality: A New Christian Ethic* (Cambridge: James Clarke, 1983), 14, 29. I cite this parenthetically as *H*.

27. Elizabeth Stuart, "Sacramental Flesh," in *Queer Theology: Rethinking the Western Body*, ed. Gerard Loughlin (Oxford: Blackwell, 2007), 68, quoting Malcolm Edwards on "eschatological erasure."

28. Mark D. Jordan, *The Invention of Sodomy in Christian Theology* (Chicago: University of Chicago Press, 1997), 163.

4. Ancestral Prophecies, Future Myths

1. "The Aesthetics of Silence" in *Susan Sontag: Essays of the 1960s and 70s*, ed. David Rieff (New York: Library of America, 2013), 292.

2. Michel Foucault, *L'herméneutique du sujet: Cours au Collège de France, 1981–1982* (Paris: Gallimard and du Seuil, 2001), 16–17.

3. Mary Daly, *Beyond God the Father: Towards a Philosophy of Women's Liberation, rev. ed.* (Boston: Beacon, 1985), 4.

4. Audre Lorde, *Zami: A New Spelling of My Name* (Watertown, MA: Persephone, 1982). I cite this volume parenthetically as *Z*.

5. This is the edition published by Crossing Press, originally in Trumansburg, New York. The phrase "a biomythography by" occurs on the cover of this later edition and several others. The key word does not occur in the body of the text.

6. Audre Lorde, *Sister Outsider: Essays and Speeches* (Trumansburg, NY: Crossing, 1984), 56–57. I cite this volume parenthetically as *SO*.

7. Audre Lorde, *I Am Your Sister: Black Women Organizing across Sexualities* (New York: Kitchen Table, 1985), 3.

8. Judy Grahn, "Why Do?," *Man-Root* 1 (August 1969): 58–60.

9. Judy Grahn, *Another Mother Tongue: Gay Words, Gay Worlds* (Boston: Beacon, 1984), 3. I cite this edition parenthetically as *AMT*.

10. The full title is "A Funeral: Plainsong from a Younger Woman to an Older Woman," in *Work of a Common Woman* (Oakland, CA: Diana, 1978; rpt. Freedom, CA: Crossing, [n.d.]). I cite this volume parenthetically as *WCW*.

11. Gloria Anzaldúa, *Borderlands/La Frontera: The New Mestiza*, 4th ed. (San Francisco: Aunt Lute Books, 2012), 33.

12. José Vasconcelos, *La raza cósmica* (Madrid: Agencia Mundial de Librería, 1925).

13. The phrase comes from an eschatological moment in Carl Wittman's "gay manifesto" (1969), originally published as "Refugees from Amerika: A Gay Manifesto." *San Francisco Free Press* (December 22, 1969–January 7, 1970), 3–5, at p. 5, col. a.

14. Mitch Walker, *Men Loving Men: A Gay Sex Guide and Consciousness Book* (San Francisco: Gay Sunshine, 1977), 147.

5. Other Regimens of Bodies and Pleasures

1. Monique Witting imagines something similar: Her women-warriors carry *feminaires* (feminaries) to record words, metaphors, ritual jokes, genital symbols, memories. Monique Wittig, *Les guérillères* (Paris: Éds. De Minuit, 1969).

2. Geoff Mains, journal entry for August 18, 1968, from his papers in the GLBT Historical Society (San Francisco), 89-3. I cite entries by the nearest date as *GMJ*.

3. For a brief history, see Gayle Rubin, "The Catacombs: A Temple of the Butthole" (1991), in *Deviations: A Gayle Rubin Reader* (Durham, NC: Duke University Press, 2011), 224–40.

4. Mains papers, in the folder "Autobiographical Notes."

5. Geoff Mains, *Urban Aboriginals: A Celebration of Leathersexuality*, pref. Mark Thompson (Los Angeles: Daedalus, 2002). I cite this edition parenthetically as *UA*.

6. Mains may have suggested "aboriginal" in posing questions.

7. Rubin, "The Catacombs," 231.

8. The last four words appear saliently in Norman O. Brown, *Love's Body* (New York: Random House, 1966).

9. Mains, *Urban Aboriginals*, 143; compare Michel Foucault, *Histoire de la sexualité*, vol. 1: *La volonté de savoir* (Paris: NRF/Gallimard, 1976), 221.

10. Mains, *Urban Aboriginals*, 133. Compare Rolland's letter of December 5, 1927, to Freud, which Freud paraphrases at the beginning of *Civilization and Its Discontents*.

11. Carlos Castañeda, *The Teachings of Don Juan: A Yaqui Way of Knowledge* (Berkeley: University of California Press, 1968), 6.

12. Quoted phrases in this paragraph come from Juicy Lucy, "If I Ask You to Tie Me Up, Will You Still Want to Love Me?," in SAMOIS Ministry of Truth, *Coming to Power . . .*, 3rd US ed. (Boston: Alyson, 1987), 31, 32, 34, 36, 38.

13. Holly Drew, "The Seduction of Earth and Rain," in *Coming to Power*, 134.

14. Pasteboards with printing master for MWMF 1977 brochure, Michigan State University Libraries, MSS 508 large.

15. Boston Women's Health Collective, *Women and Their Bodies: A Course* (Boston: WCHC, 1970), 17.

16. Sally Gearhart, *Wanderground: Tales of the Hill Women* (Watertown, MA: Persephone, 1978).

17. David Toop, *Ocean of Sound: Ambient Sound and Radical Listening in the Age of Communication* (London: Serpent's Tail, 2018), 24.

6. Pulp Poetics

1. Joan Fry, "'Congratulations! You've Just Won $295,000!': An Interview with Octavia E. Butler," *Poets and Writers*, March/April 1997, reprinted in *Conversations with Octavia Butler* (Jackson: University Press of Mississippi, 2010).

2. Robert F. Reid-Pharr, "An Interview with Samuel R. Delany," *Callaloo* 14, no. 2 (Spring 1991): 524–34.

3. Samuel R. Delany, *Trouble on Triton: An Ambiguous Heterotopia* (Middletown, CT: Wesleyan University Press, 1996), iii. In the 1976 Bantam edition, the main title is *Triton*, and the subtitle appears only on the verso of a half-title page.

4. Delany quotes from Michel Foucault, *The Order of Things: An Archeology of the Human Sciences* (New York: Pantheon, 1971), xviii.

5. In his notes to "The Waste Land," Eliot describes Tiresias as "the most important personage in the poem, uniting all the rest" (note 218). Not only Eliot: see Apollinaire's *Les mamelles de Tirésias*, Pound's *Cantos* 1, the basic conceit of Woolf's *Orlando*, and so on.

6. I quote from the later edition, Samuel Delany, *Babel-17 / Empire Star* (New York: Vintage, 2001).

7. The version of the novel originally published had suffered some cuts. They do not affect what I am about to say. The passages mentioned here can be found, as presented, in Delany's original.

8. I cannot find that the lines from "Quartet" (59) and "Electra" (187) were published by Hacker elsewhere.

9. With one exception: Wong quotes two lines of one of her own poems, "Advice to Those Who Would Love Poets." I suspect that the lines are Delany's own.

10. Samuel R. Delany, *In Search of Silence: The Journals of Samuel R. Delany*, vol. 1: 1957–1969, ed. Kenneth R. James (Middletown, CT: Wesleyan University Press, 2017), 299, "early spring 1965." There are samples of the language from another notebook, 274–80. In it, the account of the language's invention is slightly different (280).

11. Samuel R. Delany, *The Motion of Light in Water: Sex and Science Fiction Writing in the East Village* (Minneapolis: University of Minnesota Press, 2004), 155–71.

12. Marilyn Hacker, "Presentation Piece," ll. 22–23: "Take another little piece of my heart now baby," as recorded on *Cheap Thrills*, released in 1968. I follow the text in *First Cities: Collected Early Poems, 1960–1979* (New York: Norton, 2003). I cite this volume parenthetically as *FC*.

13. Marilyn Hacker, *Love, Death, and the Changing of the Seasons* (New York: Norton, 1995), xi. I cite this edition parenthetically as *LD*. The other epigraph extracts the last lines of a poem from Ezra Pound's *Cathay*, a modernist monument that inspired not a little queer poetry—say, the experiments by Amy Lowell already mentioned.

14. The phrase is controversial because poetry is usually called "lesbian" by some analogous relation to an identity. Both the identity and the relation are left unclear.

15. There are queer poetic traditions we still cannot discuss, much less praise. For example, the "Uranian" poets write ethereally, piously, but still too frankly for us about adolescent beauty.

7. Sex Beyond

1. Mark Thompson, "Introduction," in *The Fire in Moonlight: Stories from the Radical Faeries, 1975–2010*, ed. Mark Thompson et al. (Granville, NY: White Crane, 2011), 15.

2. An official biography can still be found on the Prosperos website, http://www.theprosperos.org/story.

3. See Lyon-Martin Papers, GLBT HS (San Francisco), 93-13, folders 160/6–7.

4. Phyllis Lyon, "Del Martin (1921–)," in *Before Stonewall: Activists for Gay and Lesbian Rights in Historical Context*, ed. Vern L. Bullough (Binghamton, NY: Harrington Park/Haworth, 2002), 164–65.

5. Marcia M. Gallo, *Different Daughters: A History of the Daughters of Bilitis and the Rise of the Lesbian Rights Movement* (New York: Carroll and Graf, 2006), 79.

6. Del Martin and Phyllis Lyon, *Lesbian / Woman* (repr. Volcano, CA: Volcano, 1991), 41.

7. John Lauritsen, *Religious Roots of the Taboo on Homosexuality: A Materialist View* (New York: the author, 1974).

8. Arthur Evans, *Witchcraft and the Gay Counterculture* (Boston: Fag Rag, 1978), 148.

9. Maggie Nelson, *The Argonauts* (Minneapolis, MN: Graywolf, 2015), 3.

10. I write "anal intercourse" as a final illustration of academic delicacy, while recognizing that *The Argonauts* desires to scatter my scruples. Inhibitions are stubborn.

11. Harry Dodge, *My Meteorite: or, Without the Random There Can Be No New Thing* (New York: Penguin, 2020).

12. Robert Glück, "Long Note on New Narrative," *Narrativity* 1 (n.d.), https://www.sfsu.edu/ https://~newlit/narrativity/issue_one /gluck.html.

13. These passages in *The Argonauts* highlight the absence of such passages in Dodge's *My Meteorite*. Dodge mentions transition in the most understated asides. They are not the story.

14. The quotation is from Leo Bersani and Adam Phillips, *Intimacies* (Chicago: University of Chicago Press, 2008), 114. This portion of the text is by Phillips.

Epilogue: The Impossibility of Being E(a)rnest

1. I borrow the word from Adam Phillips—who has already been cited by Maggie Nelson at the end of *The Argonauts* (Minneapolis, MN: Graywolf, 2015).

2. What Hedwig actually says, to a bed partner who has just touched their/her/his genitals, is "It's what I have to work with." *Hedwig and the Angry Inch*, dir. John Cameron Mitchel (2001).

Index

power *(continued)*
useful to, 101; enjambments of, 188; eluding, 101; invisible, 63; medical, 14, 54, 85, 95, 100, 112, 114, 137, 142; language and, 103, 128; poetry and, 132; sedimentation of, 97; sexual protest and, 180; spiritual, 179; strange, 137
powers, invisible, 63
Preston, John, 215n14
pronouns and gender, 161, 168, 185–86
Prosperos, 178–79
Proust, Marcel, 51, 56, 58, 208n11. See also *Sodom and Gomorrah*
Pynchon, Thomas, 159–60

Queensberry, Marquess of (John Sholto Douglas), 5
queer (term): fictional characters as, 63; languages and names, 11, 14; on menu of names, 13; positivism and, 14; protest against literalism, 12–13; theory and, 31
queer callings: meanings, 19. *See also* vocation

race (term): as analogy for sex/gender, 52, 55–56, 98; Black, 126, 128, 155, 188; change of, 161; embodiment and, 126; human, 100; hybrid, 135, 164; identity and, 100, 196, 209n16, 213n5; Jews as, 55, 71; language and, 26, 95; stigmatization and, 100, 135, 141; various meanings of, 135
Radical Faeries, 177–78, 182
Ram Dass (Richard Alpert), 182–83
Ramer, Andrew, 181–82
Ramsey, Frank, 29
Reid, Anthony, 176

religion: condemnation by, 85, 101; historical influence of, 98; "Old," 130–31; queerness and, 97–98, 102–3
revolution (term), 31, 42, 73, 81–83, 106–7, 121–22, 132, 162, 176, 179, 197–201
Rimbaud, Arthur, 167, 174
Rich, Adrienne, 131–32
rituals: baptism, 4; coming out, 10; concert, 131; creation of complex characters in, 137; Daly and, 124; Grahn and, 131–32; Mains and, 140–42, 145; political activity and, 183; religiosity and, 102; scandal and, 138; sexual, 106; spirituality and, 138, 181; trans, 14
Rolland, Romain, 145
Rubin, Gayle, 144, 218n3

SAMOIS (collective), 146–47
Sappho, 173
Saslow, James, 183
Schuyler, James, 187
science fiction: conventions of pulp genres, 167–69; Delany and, 160–69; exploration of sex/gender in, 150, 158–61
Scott Moncrieff, C. K., 51
secrets, 28, 57, 61, 100, 131, 138, 145–46, 158, 162, 164, 168
Sedgwick, Eve Kosofsky: *A Dialogue on Love*, 34–37, 88, 93; *Epistemology of the Closet*, 14, 30–31, 213n5; *Fat Art / Thin Art*, 34; Foucault and, 31; Heidegger and, 32; James and, 33; Merrill and, 207nn10–11; Nelson and, 187; "Pedagogy of Buddhism," 31–32, 35, 36; Proust and, 208n11; sexuality and creative interests, 35–37; *Touching Feeling*, 30–33, 37; Wittgenstein and, 30, 76

Mark Jordan is R. R. Niebuhr Research Professor at Harvard Divinity School. He has written chiefly on gender studies, Christian theology, and European philosophy. During the last few years, he has taught courses on the Western traditions of Christian soul-shaping, the relations of religion to art or literature, and the prospects for sexual ethics. His recent books include *Recruiting Young Love: How Christians Talk about Homosexuality* (2011) and *Convulsing Bodies: Religion and Resistance in Foucault* (2015). He is also the author of the groundbreaking work *The Invention of Sodomy in Christian Theology* (1997).